Rug Hooking Presents

HOOKING WITH
YARN

EDITION VII of *RUG HOOKING*
MAGAZINE'S FRAMEWORK SERIES

by Judy Taylor

Editor
Wyatt R. Myers

Book Designer
Cher WIlliams

Assistant Editor
Lisa McMullen

Photography
Judy Taylor
Impact Xpozures

Chairman
M. David Detweiler

Publisher
J. Richard Noel

Presented by

R·U·G
HOOKING

1300 Market St., Suite 202

Lemoyne, PA 17043-1420

(717) 234-5091

(800) 233-9055

www.rughookingonline.com

rughook@paonline.com

PRINTED IN CHINA

4 —
5/25

CONTENTS

D1793231

WHAT IS RUG HOOKING? — 2

ABOUT THE PUBLISHER — 3

EDITOR'S NOTE — 3

SERENDIPITY: AN INTRODUCTION TO HOOKING WITH YARN — 4

CHAPTER ONE: WHAT IS YARN? — 7

CHAPTER TWO: THE RIGHT YARN FOR THE JOB — 9

CHAPTER THREE: THE BASICS OF YARN HOOKING — 14

CHAPTER FOUR: WHICH BACKING TO USE? — 21

CHAPTER FIVE: EXPLORATIONS IN COLOR — 23

CHAPTER SIX: PRIMITIVE RUGS — 28

CHAPTER SEVEN: DYEING YARN FOR SHADING, FLOWERS, LEAVES, AND SCROLLS — 32

CHAPTER EIGHT: OTHER COLOR EFFECTS: BLENDING MULTI-COLORED YARN AND OVERDYEING — 37

CHAPTER NINE: LEFTOVER YARN FROM OLD PROJECTS — 43

CHAPTER TEN: FINISHING YOUR RUG — 46

CHAPTER ELEVEN: CARE, CLEANING, AND REPAIR — 49

CHAPTER TWELVE: HOOKING OTHER TYPES OF PROJECTS — 52

CHAPTER THIRTEEN: FOUR PROJECTS FOR YOU TO TRY — 55

SOURCES — 63

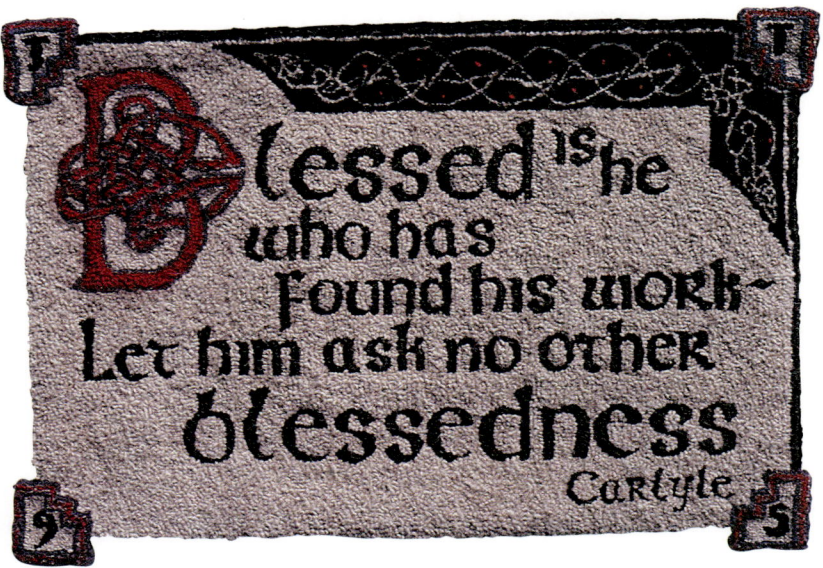

Blessed Rug, 29 ¹/2" x 20", hand-spun wool and mohair yarn on linen. Designed and hooked by Judy Taylor, Auburn, Washington, 1995.

To Gary
And to Pat and Gene

WHAT IS RUG HOOKING?

Some strips of wool. A simple tool. A bit of burlap. How ingenious were the women and men of ages past to see how such humble household items could make such beautiful rugs?

Although some form of traditional rug hooking has existed for centuries, this fiber craft became a fiber art only in the last 150 years. The fundamental steps have remained the same: A pattern is drawn onto a foundation, such as burlap or linen. A zigzag line of stitches is sewn along the foundation's edges to keep them from fraying as the rug is worked. The foundation is then stretched onto a frame, and fabric strips or yarn, which may have been dyed by hand, are pulled through it with an implement that resembles a crochet hook inserted into a wooden handle. The compacted loops of wool remain in place without knots or stitching. The completed rug may have its edges whipstitched with cording and yarn as a finishing touch to add durability.

Despite the simplicity of the basic method, highly intricate designs can be created with it. Using a multitude of dyeing techniques to produce unusual effects, or various hooking methods to create realistic shading, or different widths of wool to achieve a primitive or formal style, today's rug hookers have gone beyond making strictly utilitarian floor coverings to also make wallhangings, vests, lampshades, purses, pictorials, portraits, and more. Some have incorporated other kinds of needlework into their hooked rugs to fashion unique and fascinating fiber art that's been shown in museums, exhibits, and galleries throughout the world.

For a good look at what contemporary rug hookers are doing with yesteryear's craft—or to learn how to hook your own rug—pick up a copy of *Rug Hooking* magazine, or visit our web site at www.rughookingonline.com. Within the world of rug hooking—and *Rug Hooking* magazine—you'll find there's a style to suit every taste and a growing community of giving, gracious fiber artists who will welcome you to their gatherings.—*Wyatt Myers*

ABOUT THE PUBLISHER

Rug Hooking magazine, the publisher of *Hooking with Yarn*, welcomes you to the rug hooking community. Since 1989 *Rug Hooking* has served thousands of rug hookers around the world with its instructional, illustrated articles on dyeing, designing, color planning, hooking techniques, and more. Each issue of the magazine contains color photographs of beautiful rugs old and new, profiles of teachers, designers, and fellow rug hookers, and announcements of workshops, exhibits, and gatherings.

Rug Hooking has responded to its readers' demand for more inspiration and information by establishing an inviting, informative website at *www.rughookingonline.com* and by publishing a number of books on this fiber art. Along with how-to pattern books and a Sourcebook listing of teachers, guilds, and schools, *Rug Hooking* has produced the competition-based book series *A Celebration of Hand-Hooked Rugs*, now in its 13th year. *Hooking with Yarn* is part of *Rug Hooking*'s popular Framework Series of in-depth educational books.

The hand-hooked rugs you'll see in *Hooking with Yarn* represent just a fragment of the incredible art that is being produced today by women and men of all ages. For more information on rug hooking and *Rug Hooking* magazine, call or write us at the address on page 1.

EDITOR'S NOTE

As fiber artists, we often think of "traditional hooked rugs" as mats hooked with strips of fabric, usually 100% wool. But Judy Taylor made me realize that traditional hooked rugs were much more than this. Our ancestors hooked rugs not just for their beauty and aesthetics, but also for their necessity and practicality. As a result, many fabrics would find their way into the fiber of a hooked rug—be it wool, cut-up clothing, or even yarn.

For many, this multimedia approach is making a real comeback in the rug hooking world. The interesting thing about this revival, however, is that today different fibers are hooked together not for necessity, but for beauty. When yarn and wool strips are used together, the result is an interesting mingling of textures, colors, and personalities that can make a rug sing.

Judy Taylor understands the importance of using different fabrics in the same project all too well, which is precisely why she proposed to write a book for us on hooking with yarn. And while I must admit that I was a bit dubious at first, Judy's passion and enthusiasm as a weaver, a dyer, and a rug hooking artist soon convinced me otherwise. When I saw Judy's finished manuscript and beautiful photographs, I immediately knew I made the right decision.

So it is with great pride that we bring you Judy Taylor's *Hooking with Yarn*, the first book ever published on this glorious and multi-faceted approach to rug hooking. I certainly hope that you find Judy's enthusiastic voice, colorful photographs, and detailed, hand-drawn illustrations provide you with everything you need to introduce yarn into your rug hooking projects.

"If yarn is the alphabet, rug hooking has given me a language."
—Judy Taylor

Even if you find yourself reluctant to set your wool strips aside, I would strongly urge you to give *Hooking with Yarn* a try. As Judy will show, using yarn in your hooked projects does not mean abandoning your preferred fabric. Rather, yarn opens new doors to blending exciting new colors and textures for a wonderful visual effect. And many of the same dyeing, designing, and color planning approaches that you apply to strips of wool will work for yarn as well. Go ahead and give it a try!

When Judy learned the art of rug hooking for the first time, she thought to herself, "If yarn is the alphabet, rug hooking has given me a language." May *Hooking with Yarn* give you a language to express your character, individuality, and beauty in your own fiber art projects!

Wyatt Myers

Serendipity: An Introduction to Hooking with Yarn

Jacob Farm Rug, 36" x 25", hand-spun and blended yarn, mohair, and wool fabric strips on linen. Designed and hooked by Judy Taylor, Auburn, Washington, 1998.

Life is full of pivotal moments, where a single decision can change everything. Faced with a choice, you go on instinct and find a new way. It was like that for me the day I met my husband, and on the days my two children were born.

I experienced two other moments in which my life unalterably changed: The first was when we bought our farm, and the second was when I discovered rug hooking.

In 1988, we bought a lovely seven-acre farm in the Green River Valley in western Washington State. While the site was quite beautiful, greenery grew

A basket of Judy's hand-spun and dyed yarn.

in abundance, and we soon realized that we needed help. Being new to farming, we did not initially realize that grass wouldn't mow itself!

After a search of livestock options, we came across an ad for Angora goats. Before running across the ad, I had never known that goats could produce a fleece to be spun into yarn. I had tried a lot of different crafts, but never spinning. I must admit that I was quite intrigued by the prospect.

Very soon after buying our goats, we also purchased a few Jacob sheep. Little did I know that I would be rewriting the book of the rest of my life that summer!

A Short Lesson in the History of Rug Hooking

Though much of the history of rug hooking is still in question, its origins arguably lie in Renaissance Europe. William Winthrop Kent, in his book *The Hooked Rug*, theorized that the craft may have been started by weavers in the 1600s. After producing cloth on the loom, they were left with hundreds of strands of yarn that were too short to be used again for weaving. Whether the loops were pulled or pushed through the backing is not known, but rug hooking soon became a handy use for leftover yarn.

Rebecca Landin hooking during Traditional Rug Hooking Week at Sauder Village in Archbold, Ohio.

PHOTOGRAPH COURTESY OF LES RUPP

While evidence can be found of hooked rugs throughout Europe, the craft really took off in the late 1700s and the 1800s in North America. With the influx of European immigrants, the appeal of rug hooking grew. People needed practical and efficient crafts to make the homestead a home, and rug hooking fit the bill. All the immigrants had to take along with them was a simple hook; the other material could be found or created in their new homeland. Grain or flour sacks could be used for the backing, yarn could be spun from the wool they produced on the farm, and worn woolen clothing or blankets could be cut into strips and used for hooking.

As this brief history lesson indicates, the initial appeal of rug hooking was due in large part to its practicality. But I believe the craft offered far more than that to the pioneers who settled this wild land. It gave them a creative outlet and a chance to express themselves. Whether their drawings were crude or fancy, their colors traditional or wild, rug hooking gave them a blank canvas into which they could pour their creativity, their hopes, and their dreams.

In the late 1800s, the Industrial Revolution changed the future of rug hooking and most other crafts forever. Almost overnight, all sorts of household goods, including rugs, could be purchased at a reasonable cost, so crafts like rug hooking began to fade away.

A few decades later, during World War II, there was a need for conservation of raw materials, and rug hooking reemerged as a creative endeavor that made use of common, everyday materials. Of course, very few people were spinning yarn in the 1940s, so most people hooked rugs using fabric strips.

Since the 1940s, rug hooking has become a well-established hobby across the United States and Canada. It has evolved into a popular means of personal expression as well as a practical pastime. Hand-hooked rugs can be found on the walls of art galleries from New York City and Washington, D.C. to Tokyo and London, as well as in museums, office buildings, libraries, and cultural centers across North America.

Jacob sheep and Angora goats on Edeldal Farm, turning grass into wool. (Notice how the coats on the Angora goats keep the mohair nice and clean prior to shearing.)

A New Twist on Rug Hooking

Many excellent books and magazines specialize in traditional rug hooking, or hooking with fabric strips. But to my knowledge, there is not one single book dedicated to "Nantucket Rug Hooking," or hooking with yarn. Continuing with their commitment of education and inspiration, *Rug Hooking* has published this unique approach to traditional rug making.

You will learn everything you need to know to get started with Nantucket Rug Hooking in the chapters of this book: getting your design onto backing, hooking techniques, hemming and finishing your rugs, caring and cleaning for your hooked treasures, and much more. You will learn all about yarn: which breeds of sheep make the best rug yarn, how yarn is made, how to dye yarn for a variety of effects, and sources for the best rug hooking yarns. You will learn about the variety of backing materials used in rug hooking, and which material is best for different types of projects.

The rest is up to you. Like a blank canvas to a painter, or language to a poet, rug hooking can give you a unique and exciting way of expressing yourself. Give it a try. But I must warn you; it could change your life!

Two years and boxes, bags, and baskets of hand-spun yarn later, I was earnestly in search of something to do with my yarn. I had tried knitting, crochet, weaving, and even macramé, but I hadn't quite found the same spark I felt when spinning yarn. Then in 1990, I discovered a Claire Murray rug shop in a little town on the Olympic Peninsula. I found myself surrounded by rugs made with thick wool yarn, just the kind I liked to spin. I took a class, and the moment I put the hook through the backing, I knew that it was time to rewrite my life's book once again.

There is just *something* about the craft of rug hooking. It is tactile, just like spinning, but it feeds the heart and soul, too. If yarn is the alphabet, rug hooking has given me a language. I have been able to express myself more creatively through the fiber art of rug hooking than ever before.

What Is Yarn?

Judy Taylor spinning wool at her spinning wheel.

A quick view of how raw wool becomes yarn. Wool samples on the left, from top to bottom: Cotswold, Romney, Jacob, Navajo, and mohair. To the right of these samples is a washed Border Leicester sample that was hand-carded, spun on a drop spindle, and plied.

In the simplest of terms, yarn is fiber that is twisted to hold it together and plied for strength. Yarn can be spun from animal fibers, such as sheep, goat, llama, alpaca, rabbit, dog, silkworm, camel, and even musk-ox.

A Culture of Spinning

Plant fibers, such as flax (linen), jute (burlap), and cotton (monk's cloth), are also spun and have been for thousands of years. Every culture in the world spins yarn, whether it is done using the ancient drop spindle, or the more modern invention of the spinning wheel (16th century).

Wool is the primary fiber used in rug hooking, although I also use a lot of wool/mohair blends in my rugs. The breeds of sheep that produce the best rug hooking wools are called "long-wools," and include Lincoln, Romney, Navajo, Border Leceister, and Cotswold. Kid mohair, the fiber of the young Angora goat, is usually used in sweaters, but the adult mohair fleece is strong and lustrous and makes a beautiful rug yarn when blended with wool. Jacob sheep naturally produce a medium-fine sweater wool, but they also produce a coarse leg wool, which is perfect for rug making.

How to Spin

Usually, the wool is washed before spinning. The fibers must be opened up, so they can be spun into a smooth, even strand. Fibers can be fluffed up with the hands or pulled apart by a picker. Then the fibers are usually brushed or carded so that they are roughly all going in the same direction. This carded wool can then be spun into yarn.

Carded wool is a fluffy mass of wool, which can easily be pulled apart, but when a little twist is applied, it becomes strong. Whether using a drop spindle or a spinning wheel, the spinner allows a small amount of carded wool to be twisted, spreading the fibers out and letting the twist travel up the fiber supply (i.e., the supply of carded wool from which you're drawing) in a long, continuous motion. When the spinner has filled two or more spindles, or bobbins, with enough yarn, multiple strands of yarn can be plied together from different bobbins to create a very strong, balanced yarn.

The spinner changes direction in the twist, depending on whether she is spinning singles or plying. Singles are usually spun using a "Z" twist. By turning the spinning wheel in a clockwise direction,

SPINNING YARN

Figure One: Fibers are plied in a uniform direction with a "Z" twist.

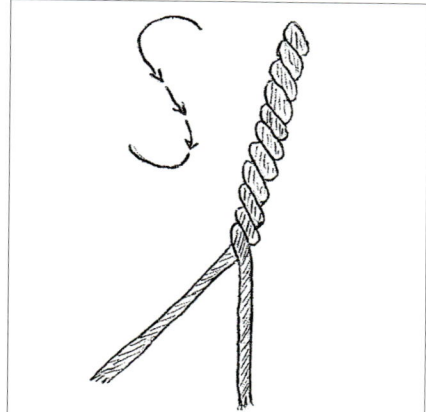

Figure Two: Two single plies are twisted in the opposite direction ("S" twist) to create a double-ply yarn.

the fiber is twisted so that the angle of the twist is the same as the diagonal line in a "Z." The fibers need to be twisted enough so that they won't fall apart, but too much twist will cause the single to kink when relaxed.

A single-ply yarn is not used very often by itself because it is not as durable as a plied yarn. Also, if you knit with a single-ply yarn, you might find that your knitted piece would tend to stretch across the bias because all of the twist in the yarn is going in one direction.

To counter this effect, yarn is created by spinning single plies in one direction ("Z" twist), and then plying them in the opposite direction ("S" twist). (In fact, it would not matter whether the singles were spun in a "Z" or an "S" twist, so long as the plying is done in the opposite direction.) The spinner takes up single plies from two or more bob-

bins, and turning the spinning wheel in a counter-clockwise direction, twists the single plies together. There is a certain amount of twist "energy," if you will, going one direction in the singles. Then, there is twist "energy" going in the opposite direction from the plying. The end product is a balanced yarn that does not kink or unravel. The spinner can ply any number of singles together. The more singles that are plied together, the stronger and more durable the yarn; a two-ply yarn is stronger than a single ply, and a three-ply yarn is stronger still.

The wool can be dyed before spinning, or the yarn itself can be dyed after spinning. Different colors also can be blended in the spinning process for a multi-colored effect. (Dyeing and blending are covered in Chapters 5 through 8.)

A basket of Judy Taylor's hand-spun, beautifully dyed yarn.

The Right Yarn for the Job

A basket of Judy's hand-spun and dyed yarn and a niddy-noddy, a funny-named tool that is used to wrap yarn into skeins and measure a uniform amount of yarn for each skein.

Buster, 31" x 18¹/₂", hand-spun wool and mohair yarn (in natural and dyed colors) on linen. Designed and hooked by Judy Taylor, Auburn, Washington, 1996.

In my years of rug hooking, I have sought inspiration from the many books and magazines on the subject. Since these publications focus mainly on traditional rug hooking (hooking with strips of wool), however, I have had to modify what I've read to apply those techniques and ideas to hooking with yarn.

Through these attempts to create my own style in yarn, I have learned some very encouraging things. I have discovered that with a few modifications, just about everything you can do with fabric strips in a hooked rug you can also do with yarn.

Why Not Use Yarn?

Yarn is just as versatile as fabric strips for rug hooking. In fact, it actually offers some advantages. It is easier to work with, stronger, and more durable. And surprisingly, some things that you can do with yarn you simply cannot do with fabric strips. So why doesn't everyone hook with yarn?

For one thing, finding good material for hooking with yarn is often a drawback. Everyone knows where to get good wool fabric for fabric strips—they either purchase it off the bolt at a fabric store, or they recycle woolen garments from thrift stores.

Good wool yarn for hooking, on the other hand, is a little harder to come by. The image that comes to mind when people think of yarn is often the acrylics sold at craft stores. Good wool yarn may be harder to find, but once you establish your sources, you can get excellent yarn whenever you need it.

Halcyon yarn

New Zealand Wool Pak

Brown Sheep Lamb's Pride Bulky Lopi, Reynolds Lopi, and Reynolds Bulky Lopi

The Right Yarn

The best yarn for rug hooking is called "bulky yarn." The label may say "bulky," "chunky," or sometimes "worsted weight." Yarn with any of these three labels will work well for rug hooking. In addition, most commercial yarns have a knitting gauge on the label. A yarn that knits $3^1/2$ to $4^1/2$ stitches per inch is a good weight for rug hooking. You can hook with finer or thicker yarns, but most of the yarn I use falls within that range. The thinner the yarn, the finer the overall look. I often use thinner yarns for the detail areas and fill in background areas with thicker yarn, so the hooking goes faster.

As I mentioned in Chapter One, longwools make the best rug hooking yarns. Unless you are buying from a hand-spinner, however, the label will not specify breeds of wool. You have to rely on your sense of touch. A good rug hooking yarn will feel coarse, even a little scratchy. If the yarn is a blend of wool and mohair, the mohair will give the yarn added strength and luster. Personally, I don't like to hook with 100% mohair. It is too slippery and lacks the loft (springiness or airiness) of a wool yarn.

My Yarns of Choice

The yarns that I use most in rug hooking are **Halycon rug wool, New Zealand Wool Pak, Reynolds Lopi, Reynolds Bulky Lopi, Brown Sheep Lamb's Pride Bulky Lopi, Rowanspun Chunky, Rowan Magpie Tweed, Peace Fleece, Ewenique, and, of course, my own hand-spun.** (See the sidebar on page 11.) These yarns range in price from $2 to $3 per ounce. I usu-

ally figure I will need 4 ounces per square foot of hooked area, which gives me a range of $8 to $12 per square foot. If you are buying wool fabric by the yard, the cost is about the same (if you figure 1 yard of wool fabric for each square foot of a hooked rug).

This is by no means a complete list of all of the great yarns for rug hooking. These are just some of the brands that I have tried, really liked, and have continued to use in my projects. But I am always on the lookout for new yarns and expect to add to this list in the future. I can recommend the following yarns because they are of excellent quality and reasonable price, but many other yarns on the market could also work just as well. (For more information on where you can purchase yarn, check out "Sources" on page 63.)

Halcyon Rug Wool: This yarn is the bulkiest of the group and is comparable to a #8-cut ($^8/_{32}$") wool strip. This yarn is only sold through mail order, but Halcyon has a myriad of beautiful colors from which to choose. Plus, if you run out of yarn, they likely will be able to send you more, as they have a large inventory of yarn available at all times.

I will often buy Halcyon in light or variegated colors and overdye it. Halcyon is great for background areas: Their yarn is so bulky that it fills in large areas quickly. But personally, I prefer using a finer yarn (such as New Zealand Wool Pak) for detail areas.

New Zealand Wool Pak: This is a plied yarn that is much finer than Halcyon. It is comparable to a #6-cut ($^6/_{32}$") wool strip. I use this yarn for dip dyeing, or anywhere that I want fine detail. It comes in a more limited range

Rowanspun Chunky and Rowan Magpie Tweed

Peace Fleece

Ewenique

of colors, but again, I buy it with the intention of dyeing it, so I usually buy white, off-white, or gray.

Reynolds Lopi, Reynolds Bulky Lopi, and Brown Sheep Lamb's Pride Bulky Lopi: Lopi is a thick, single-ply yarn. The width of these yarns ranges from the equivalent of a #6 cut ($^6/_{32}$") to a #8 cut ($^8/_{32}$") in fabric strips. They come in a beautiful array of colors and are very easy to hook with, so I often use them in my rug hooking classes. A single-ply yarn, however, is not as durable as a plied yarn, so I often use these Lopi yarns in pillows, stuffed animals, or wallhangings, but not in floor rugs.

Rowanspun Chunky and Rowan Magpie Tweed: These are considered bulky knitting yarns, which compare to a #4 cut ($^4/_{32}$") of fabric strips. They don't come in a wide range of colors, but they are usually tweedy and variegated in both texture and color. They are among the most expensive of rug hooking yarns, but they are truly lovely, almost hand-spun looking. Plus, they overdye beautifully.

Peace Fleece: Another delightful

Some Good Yarns for Rug Hooking

Below are samples of rug hooking yarn that Judy commonly uses in her projects. They are:

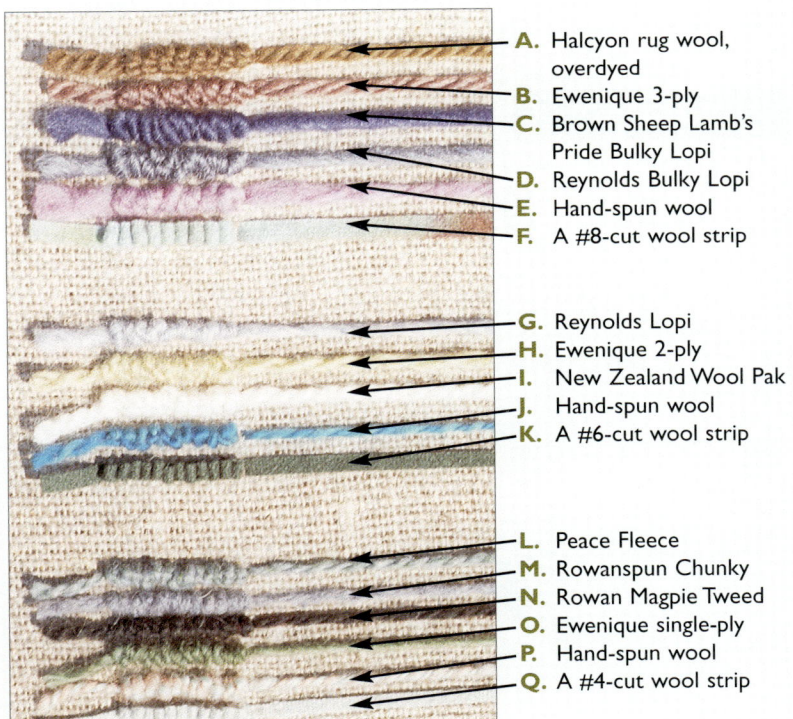

A. Halcyon rug wool, overdyed
B. Ewenique 3-ply
C. Brown Sheep Lamb's Pride Bulky Lopi
D. Reynolds Bulky Lopi
E. Hand-spun wool
F. A #8-cut wool strip

G. Reynolds Lopi
H. Ewenique 2-ply
I. New Zealand Wool Pak
J. Hand-spun wool
K. A #6-cut wool strip

L. Peace Fleece
M. Rowanspun Chunky
N. Rowan Magpie Tweed
O. Ewenique single-ply
P. Hand-spun wool
Q. A #4-cut wool strip

Notice how these different types of yarns match the corresponding widths of different popular cuts of wool strips. Also note that the thinner the yarn, the closer together the loops become to fill in the same space. The loops, however, are still all the same height.

Hand-spun yarn

yarn with lots of character is Peace Fleece. Like the Rowan yarns, Peace Fleece resembles hand-spun yarns in color and texture. Available in dyed and blended colors, Peace Fleece is a plied yarn spun with coarse wool. It is a worsted weight, so it compares to a #4 ($^4/_{32}$") in fabric strips.

Ewenique: This is a commercially spun yarn that I have made especially for rug hooking, using wool and mohair from my own flock. I called upon my experience as a hand-spinner and rug hooker to design a yarn that is perfect for rug hooking, and "Ewenique" was the result. It is thin enough to pull smoothly through the backing, yet it is lofty enough to fill in areas quickly. Also, the mohair gives the yarn added strength, which is so important in rug hooking, as well as a little luster and

shine, which I really like. Ewenique is a blend of 65% wool and 35% mohair. I ply it myself on my spinning wheel, so I can determine whether I want a 2-ply, a bulky 3-ply, or sometimes I use singles for fine detail. It is naturally gray, but the mohair content allows me to overdye for a beautiful range of colors. I sell Ewenique, both in the natural gray, and hand-dyed in a whole range of colors (except white). (To order Judy's Ewenique yarn, see the "Sources" section on page 63.)

Having your own fleece spun by a mill for rug hooking yarn can be a great source for your projects, but since most mills require a minimum run of 50 pounds, some small flock owners might not be able to take advantage of this option.

Hand-spun: The beauty of hand-

CREATING A GAUGE

Figure One: Hook a 3" x 3" square.

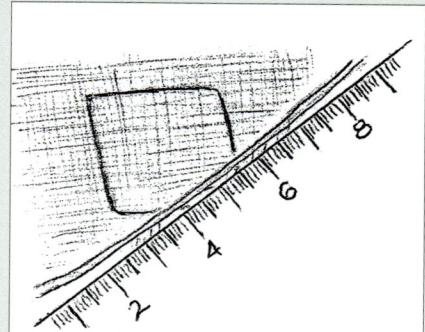

Figure Two: Pull out the yarn and measure its length.

Gauging Your Yarn Needs

When planning my rug projects, I need to make a rough estimate of how much yarn I will need. One way I have found to do this is with a "gauge." The process is very simple, and I have found a gauge to be a very useful tool in determining how much yarn I need. Here is how you do it:

1) Draw a 3" x 3" square on your backing.

2) Hook the area, pull it out, and measure the yarn.

3) Divide the number of feet you used to hook the square by nine, and you will know how many feet you used per square inch.

4) Based on this gauge, I usually estimate that I will need 4 ounces of yarn per square foot of hooked area (background), or 2 feet per square inch (detail areas).

Of course, one can never know exactly how much yarn will be needed until the rug is hooked. First of all, we are estimating roughly the square footage of a given area. Then as we hook, we continually make decisions that may affect how much yarn we will use in that area. Part of the fun of rug hooking for me is in improvising when I think I might be short on a certain yarn. Sometimes the best ideas come to me when I am brainstorming to avoid running out of a color. I might decide to create a new design element to fill up space, or gradually eliminate the short color by incorporating another color in a background area. These decisions add something special to the project.

Judy's niddy-noddy.

spun yarn is that you are truly starting your project from scratch. You get to make every decision: which fibers to use, how thick you want the yarn, whether you want to use natural colors or dye, whether you want to dye the wool first or dye the yarn, and the list goes on and on.

You certainly do not need to learn to spin in order to hook with hand-spun yarn. One of the best ways to find hand-spinners is to visit a local spinning guild meeting. There, you will find a group of hand-spinners that are probably just as eager to find out about rug hooking as you are about finding sources of hand-spun yarn. You also may be able to find spinners' events that take place in your area, where hand-spun yarn can be purchased.

I use all types of yarn in my projects, but people seem to be really attracted to the hand-spun ones most of all. They may not even be aware that the yarn was hand-spun, but just find the unique texture, color, and blend especially appealing.

The Basics of Yarn Hooking

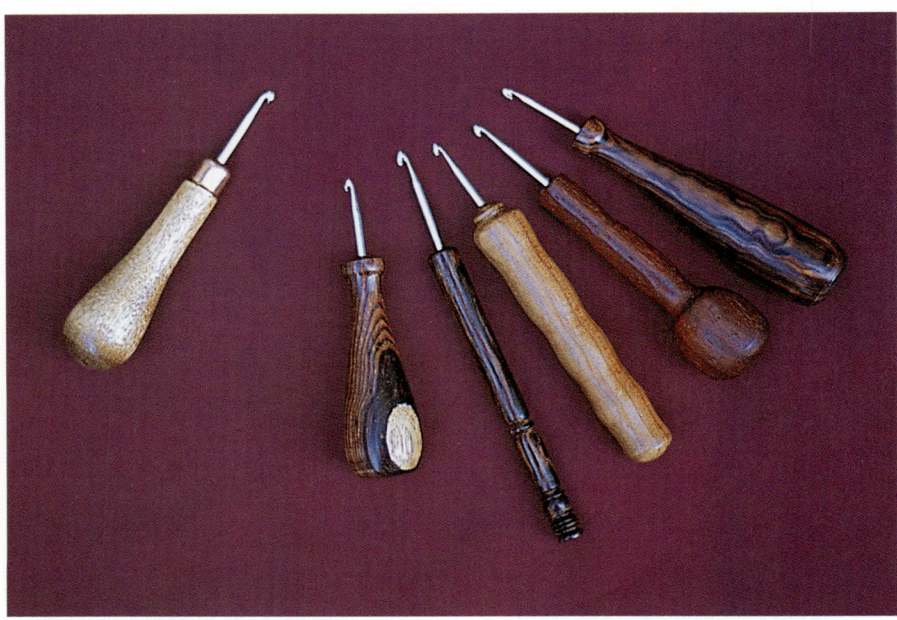

Hooks: Pine-handled hook on the left, assorted hand-made hardwood handles on the right.

The first rug hook was probably a nail, with the point bent to form a hook. Nowadays, most rug hooks are made with a standard crochet hook, which is cut short and mounted in a wooden handle so that it is easy to hold in your fist. Hooks range in price from $6 to $30 and vary in size from fine to primitive.

Hooked on the Options

My favorite hook size is called "coarse." It is one size down from the largest hook (primitive), and compares to a size "0" in a standard crochet hook. With this hook, I can comfortably hook everything from Halcyon rug wool to wool embroidery thread. A coarse rug hook connects easily with the yarn and also pulls smoothly through linen or burlap backing. The only time I like to use a smaller hook is if I use a backing fabric with a tighter weave (such as counted cross-stitch fabric).

Once you have decided what size hook you want, you can choose the size and type of handle. You could opt for the manufactured pine-handled hooks, which are inexpensive and utilitarian, or you could pay a little more for hand-made hardwood handles in every imaginable size, shape, and price. Some hooks have metal handles as well, which I have yet to find for sale in my local craft or fabric stores. Many companies, however, sell metal-handled hooks through the mail. (Many of these suppliers are listed in the "Sources" section on page 63.)

Yarn vs. Fabric Strips

The main difference in the hooking technique between yarn and fabric strips is that yarn is pretty tough and can withstand being pulled up and down through the backing. This simple truth allows the hooker to build up considerable speed, especially when hooking solid-colored areas. This also means that yarn can be re-hooked over and over again, so you can change your mind about a particular design, color, or hooking style if you'd like.

On the other hand, fabric strips are cut on the edges, and even if the fabric is well felted, the strips can fray on the edges if handled too roughly. If you want to hook with fabric strips, avoid the step (Figure 2 on page 15) where you give yourself that extra slack, and con-

Hooking Technique

1. The best way to start hooking with yarn is to put the backing, design side up, on your lap.

2. With your knees comfortably apart (approximately 9" to 10"), tuck the backing under your legs. Your legs then become your "frame."

3. Take the end of a ball of yarn in your left hand, underneath the backing. With the hook above in your right hand, push in the hook where you want to begin. (If you are left-handed, reverse.)

4. Connect the yarn onto the hook underneath the backing, and pull the end through to the top. Leave about 1" of yarn on the top for the time being. (You will get rid of this end later.)

Figure 1

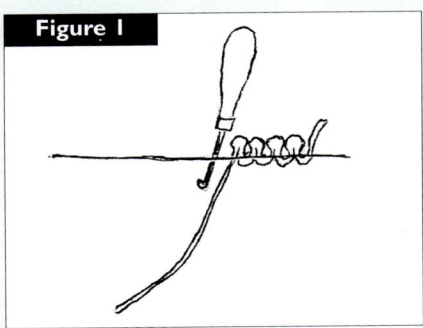

5. Push your hook in the backing, close to the end that you just brought up, and let your left hand slide down the yarn a few inches so that you give yourself a little bit of slack in the yarn. (See Figure 1 above.)

6. Connect the yarn to the hook with your left hand, and continue to give downward pressure on the yarn with your left hand until you have drawn the yarn up to the topside of the backing. (See Figure 2 above.)

Figure 2

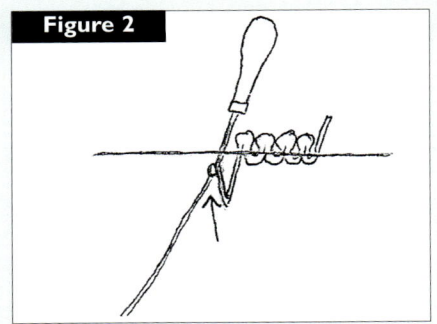

Figure 3

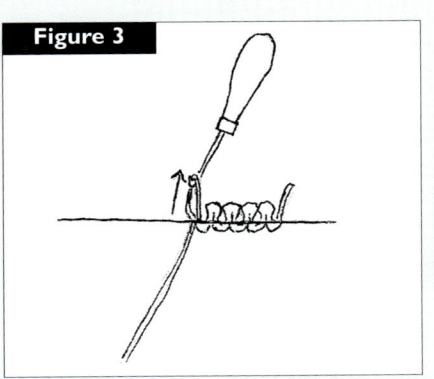

7. Then, as you continue to pull up on the rest of the slack with your right hand, feel with your left hand to make sure the yarn is pulled snug up to the back of the rug. (See Figure 3 above.)

Figure 4

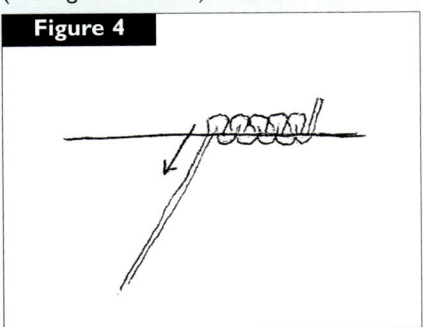

8. Then with your left hand, pull the loop down to the desired height (approximately 1/4"). (See Figure 4 above.)

9. Please note that hooking with yarn is slightly different than hooking with strips of fabric. (See Figure 5 above.) As you can see, you can easily pull out your previous loop if you don't give yourself adequate

Figure 5

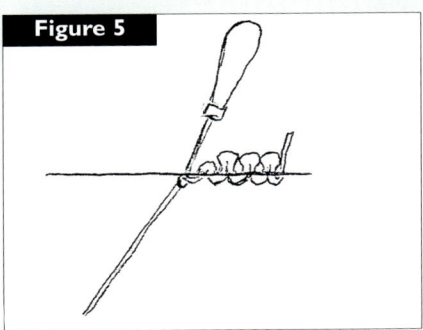

slack between loops, and then pull the slack tight between loops. This may seem like a bit of extra work, but trust me: It's really easy to get the hang of it. And it's a small price to pay for the extra beauty and texture of yarn in your piece!

Figure 6

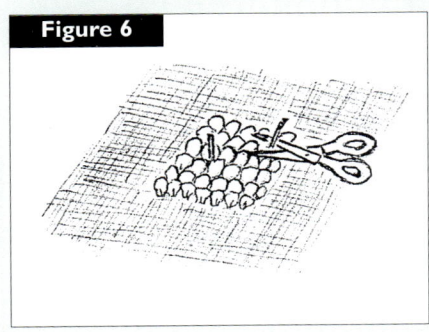

10. Following this same process, hook each successive loop. When you come to the end of a section of color, push in your hook just as if you were going to make another loop. When you have pulled the loop all the way up on the top, you can cut it on the top of the rug rather than making another loop. Leave about 1" sticking up, just like you did at the beginning of the section, and pull the rest of the yarn out through the back. These ends, once surrounded by loops, can be cut off level with the surface of the rug. (See Figure 6 above.)

Judy hooking in the traditional Nantucket style, using her lap as the hooking frame.

nect the fabric strip to your hook very close to the loop before it. Then gently pull the loop through to the top. (Look at Figure 5 on page 15 once again. This step that we discourage for hooking with yarn is common practice for hooking with strips.)

The other big difference between fabric and yarn is the shape. Yarn is round and will pull snug against the back of the rug. With fabric strips, however, you must take care not to let the strip twist in the backing, as this will leave a bump that could catch on something later, pulling out some of your loops.

A Few Extra Hints on Yarn Hooking

Now that you understand the basic methods of hooking with yarn and

Getting Your Design to Backing

You never know when the inspiration for a design might hit you. Quilt patterns, Celtic patterns, pictorials, and abstracts all may catch your eye and make you begin planning a rug. For every person who makes a rug, an infinite number of designs are out there, and no two people will do the same design in the same way. But many would-be designers face a common problem: How do you get your brilliant idea to materialize into a rug?

First get your design on paper, preferably paper that is big enough to accommodate the whole rug. By starting with a paper and pencil, you can erase and redraw until the design is just the way you want it. Then go over your pencil with a Sharpie pen or permanent marker.

The very best method I've found for transferring my paper design to linen is to draw it on window screening (this can be purchased by the roll at a hardware store). Lay the window screen over your paper design and simply trace over all the lines with your Sharpie pen, so that the exact copy is transferred to the window screen.

Transferring a paper design to a window screen.

Transferring the design from window screen to linen backing.

Then lay the window screen over your linen backing, and repeat the process, drawing over all the lines. Remove the window screen and redraw the lines if they are too faint. The window screen can be re-used over and over, which is great for me, since I sell my patterns. But even if it is only used once, it is the best way to get your design accurately transferred to your backing.

Some people find it intimidating to draw their designs with permanent marker because they may be unsure about the design that they want. Just remember that whatever you draw with the Sharpie pen is not going to show on the finished rug. You can change your mind and change the pattern later. But you need to start with a permanent marker so that the ink will not bleed into the rug later when it is washed, or rub off during the hooking process.

You can also purchase designs drawn on the backing of your choice. In the "Sources" section on page 63, you will find listings of many companies who market their own patterns.

how the process differs from hooking with fabric strips, you should be just about ready to hook! Before you get started, however, please refer to the hints below.

Placing your loops: How far apart you place your loops depends upon the thickness of the yarn. A good rule of thumb is that you want your loops close enough together so you cannot see the backing from the top, but not so close together that the rug will not lie flat. The guiding principle in rug hooking is that you are drawing a thick yarn through a very small hole, so naturally, the loop spreads out above the hole. As you pack more and more loops into the top of the rug, an outward pressure radiates from each individual loop, giving a lushness and fullness to the project as a whole.

Notice the weave on your backing material. Unless I am hooking with a very fine yarn, I hook about every other hole in the weave (the finer the yarn, the closer the loops). This gives the loops sufficient room to spread and allows me to pack loops together for maximum durability. The only way you can tell if you are over-packing your loops is if you have hooked a large enough section. Untuck the edges of the fabric, and let the rug relax. If it tends to curl on the hooked edges, you are putting your loops too closely together.

This is a leap of faith for some beginners. As you get used to working with yarn, you begin to trust that these loops can be packed in such a way that they will stay put without over-packing.

Different types of yarn in the same project: I often work with a variety of yarns in the same project. Some

Some samples of Judy's hand-spun and dyed yarn.

yarns may be hand-spun, some commercially spun, and I sometimes incorporate fabric strips into the same project as well. The thing to keep in mind when combining yarns of different weights, or yarn and fabric strips, is to keep your loops at a uniform height. Generally, my loops are no higher than $1/4$". Short, densely packed loops will wear better in a floor rug, so I try to make my loops about as short as I can without pulling them all the way through to the back. If you are making a wallhanging, you can play around more with different heights and textures, but it is best to learn to make your loops short and densely packed for floor rugs.

The thinner the yarn, the closer I will need to place the loops. Again, following the basic rule of thumb, I want the loops close enough together so that I cannot see the backing from the front. As long as the loops are all the same height, I can switch easily from thick

TO FRAME OR NOT TO FRAME?

Frames: From top to bottom: embroidery frame, carding cloth frame, PVC frame, and scroll frame. (*Note the extra material sewn on the sides of the* Crown of Thorns *rug, so I can hook the project away from home on my lap.*)

around with me everywhere I go.

On the other hand, I also like to have a rug project set up on my frame at home. If I have to get up to answer the phone, I can walk away from the rug without having to unwind myself from it. A frame also has advantages when I am hooking on a hot summer day. A wool rug can be stifling wrapped around your legs when the temperature rises! A frame also allows me to change position while hooking, which helps me avoid fatigue.

Your Framing Options

Frame designs differ in the way they hold onto the backing fabric. With a **scroll frame,** the backing is rolled onto a dowel on both ends. With an **embroidery frame** or a **PVC frame,** the backing is clamped onto the frame. In addition, a **carding cloth frame** allows you to stretch your backing over tiny nails on the edges of the frame. Each of these designs has its advantages and disadvantages.

Scroll Frame

A scroll frame can be purchased at most craft stores. One advantage of the scroll frame is that it has side mountings that allow you to keep both hands free for rug hooking. With a scroll frame, however, you are limited by the width. Your scroll frame would have to be wide enough to

One of the features that distinguishes Nantucket Rug Hooking from the traditional style is the fact that you do not need a frame; the backing fabric can simply be tucked around your legs. If you prefer to use a frame, however, you have plenty of options from which to choose.

Dozens of frames are available: Some designed for quiltmaking and others made especially for rug hooking. These range from a simple embroidery hoop to a floor model frame to accommodate large rugs.

Whether or not you use a frame is a matter of individual taste. I alternate equally between hooking on a frame and hooking in my lap, depending on where I am. If I want to take a rug project with me, nothing could be easier than throwing the backing and yarn in a bag. Then anywhere that I can sit down, I can hook. I really enjoy the convenience of not having to lug a frame

accommodate your entire project, which could prove cumbersome for a larger rug. The larger the project, the larger your frame will have to be.

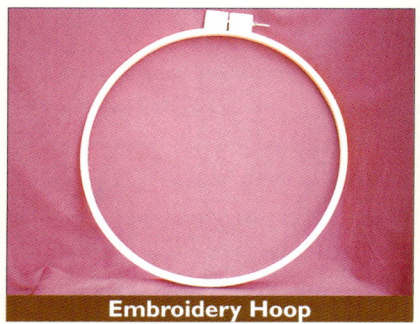

Embroidery Hoop

An embroidery hoop is also commonly available and very inexpensive. Unless it is mounted in some way, however, it can be awkward. You need both hands free for rug hooking. Also, an embroidery hoop cannot be clamped over the hooked area, so you are again limited by size with an embroidery hoop.

PVC Frame

I designed a simple rug frame that I like using PVC piping. The frame is of table height, at which I can comfortably sit. It uses clamps on both sides, which makes the setup quite similar to wrapping the backing around my legs. Since I cannot clamp over the hooked area, however, I designed the frame to be wide enough to accommodate most large rugs. This frame can be easily taken apart and moved, but I

prefer to set it up and leave it in one place.

Carding Cloth Frame

Another frame designed especially for rug hooking is the carding cloth frame, which holds onto the backing fabric using tiny nails or carding cloth. It is mounted so that it can sit on a table or stand on the floor, and it is collapsible so that it can be portable. The backing fabric is stretched across the frame and held in place with tiny nails. The advantage of this design is that you are not at all limited in the size of the project. The nails can hold onto the hooked area as well as the backing, so you can move a large rug around as needed. You need to be careful when moving the hooked rug around on the carding cloth frame, as the tiny nails can sometimes snag the loops in the areas that you have already hooked.

Frames range in price from a couple of dollars for an embroidery frame to over a hundred dollars for the top of the line specialty frames. The nice thing about Nantucket Rug Hooking is that you can learn to hook on your lap. Then if you decide that you love the craft but would prefer to use a frame, you can find the frame that best suits your needs and pocketbook. You will find many companies listed in the "Sources" section on page 63 that sell frames for rug hooking.

yarns to thin yarns or fabric strips. (See photo on page 11.)

Hints for beginners: There are two common problems that arise for beginners: One is the tendency to connect with only part of the yarn on the hook, thereby splitting the yarn. The other is accidentally pulling out the previous loop when moving on to the next.

To avoid splitting the yarn on your hook, remind yourself to keep control of the slack yarn with your left hand, until you pull your hook through to the front of the backing. I continue to give downward pressure on the yarn with my left hand until the yarn has been pulled through to the front. Then, I feel with my left hand to make sure I'm pulling all the way up on the slack. That way, I can be sure the yarn is snug up against the back.

A two-step process: When I pull up on the yarn, I am thinking about the back of the rug. Then when I pull the loop down to the desired height, I'm thinking about the top. By breaking the process down into these steps, I can get good consistency and surprising speed. If ever I find that I am splitting the yarn, I just try to remind myself to keep downward pressure on the yarn with my left hand.

The importance of slack: If you find that you are pulling out the previous loop, check and see that you are giving yourself enough slack in the yarn. If you are connecting the yarn onto the hook too closely to the previous loop, then it is easy to pull out the loop before it.

When I first push my hook into the backing, my left hand is pushing up on the backing from below, giving me something to push against. But then my left hand slides down the yarn, so that the point where I am connecting the yarn on the hook is actually several inches from where the yarn came out the back at the previous loop. That way, I have several inches to pull up before I could pull out the last loop.

At the same time, my left hand is feeling underneath, to make sure I'm pulling the extra yarn all the way up. As soon as I feel the yarn pull tight across the back, I stop pulling up, to avoid pulling out the last loop.

Re-hooking

When I am demonstrating or teaching rug hooking, the concept that sometimes gives students the most trouble is the idea that yarn can be pulled out of the rug at any time. What may seem like a disadvantage to a beginning rug hooker is actually the main feature that gives hooked rugs such longevity! Also, the fact that I can pull out yarn gives me the freedom to experiment, re-hooking until I get the rug just the way I want it.

Often I don't know exactly what I want until I see it hooked. Sometimes colors that look great together in skeins look muddy when hooked side by side. Other times my first attempt to create a design element doesn't look quite right.

One of the great things about hooking with yarn is that I can pull out the yarn in that particular section and re-hook it or replace it with something different without having to undo any more of the rug. This is something that I find particularly frustrating about knitting and weaving. If I make a mistake, I have to un-knit or un-weave all the way back to the mistake, wasting all my efforts! So if you are not happy with a hooked area, feel free to pull out the yarn and re-hook until it's the way you envisioned.

A well-made hooked rug can last 100 to 200 years. Crucial to the longevity of these rugs is the fact that they can be re-hooked. If you think about it, a rug that has been on the floor and used for a generation or two is bound to need repairs at some point. The rug may get stained, moth-eaten, or heavily worn in one particular high-traffic spot. The damaged area of the rug can be un-hooked and replaced, thereby extending the life of the rug. (Repair of hooked rugs is covered in Chapter 11.)

Antique Flower Chairpad, 14" in diameter, New Zealand Wool Pak and Brown Sheep Lopi on burlap. Designed and hooked by Judy Taylor, Auburn, Washington, 2001.

Which Backing to Use?

Several different backing fabrics are used in rug hooking, and burlap, linen, and monk's cloth are among the most popular. Your choice of backing fabric is going to depend on the type of project. Each fabric has unique qualities that make it suitable for different uses. All of them are made with a fairly open weave, which is roomy enough to poke through easily with your hook but tight enough to hold the yarn in loops.

Burlap

Burlap: The key difference between burlap, linen, and monk's cloth is the fiber from which they are made. Burlap is made from jute, linen from flax, and monk's cloth from cotton. Jute is a fiber that can rot when it gets wet. When we plant trees, the root ball is wrapped in burlap. The burlap biodegrades as the tree grows. As a result, burlap is not suitable for floor rugs, which will need to be washed.

Linen: On the other hand, the flax plant, when it is prepared for spinning, is soaked in water, and everything that doesn't rot is spun into linen. So a floor rug hooked on linen is rot-resistant, durable, and will last for generations.

Monk's Cloth: Cotton monk's cloth is also washable, but cotton fibers are

Backing fabrics: The teddy bear has burlap in its lap, the Celtic Vest is lying on top of a piece of white monk's cloth, and the pattern for the *Star Rug* is drawn on linen. All items designed and hooked by Judy Taylor.

fairly short and brittle, so cotton fabric wears out sooner. Monk's cloth can be purchased starched or unstarched. The unstarched monk's cloth is much softer and more lightweight than linen or burlap, so I like to use it for garments. That way my backing fabric does not add too much bulk to the garment, and since I am hooking with wool, I know the garment will be gently worn and washed. The backing fabric used in a hooked garment will not have to undergo the same wear and tear as a floor rug.

The Economics of Backing Fabrics

There is a considerable price difference among backing fabrics. Burlap is relatively inexpensive and can

Linen

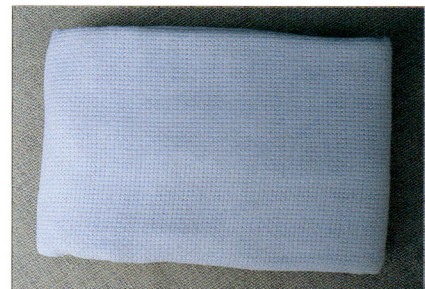

Monk's Cloth

be purchased at any fabric store for around $3 a yard. Monk's cloth is a little harder to find, but some stores sell it for around $12 a yard. Linen rug backing is not sold in ordinary fabric stores because it is not used for anything else except rug hooking, but linen can be purchased from rug hooking companies for around $22 a yard. (Check out the "Sources" section on page 63 to find companies that sell backing fabrics.)

Value: I only use linen in floor rugs. The fabric is more expensive, but you get what you pay for. If you think about it, the real value of a hooked rug is not

in the cost of the backing fabric or the yarn. What is considered most when pricing a hooked rug is time. I will put exactly the same labor into a rug whether I hook it on burlap or linen. The burlap rug would save me $19 a yard, but it might only last through 20 years of regular wear and tear. The same rug hooked on linen could last 100 to 200 years. With linen backing, I can confidently assure my customers that the rug has not only beauty, but also lasting quality.

When I draw my design on burlap backing, I always leave about 18" of fabric on the sides, so that I will have something to wrap around my legs. Linen, on the other hand, is more expensive, so to avoid wasting the precious cloth, I draw my pattern using the maximum area of the piece of linen, leaving about 4" all around for a hem, and then I sew extra fabric on the sides to wrap around my legs. This way I am making the best use of the linen that I can without waste. By sewing fabric on the sides, I can take the rug off the frame to work on it away from home in my lap.

Burlap is great for pillows, stuffed animals, decorations, or any other type of project that will not need to be washed regularly. Burlap is suitable for wallhangings as well, since they will not need to be washed. If it were a very special project that I wanted to last forever, however, I still would use linen. Again, I am going to put the same amount of labor into the project, so why scrimp on the backing fabric?

No Latex Backing!

I am often asked if I use any kind of additional backing on my rugs to hold them together. The answer is absolutely not! A well-hooked rug will not need anything to hold it together. The loops will stay in place through vacuuming, washing, and normal wear and tear. If the occasional loop should get snagged, it can easily be re-hooked.

The problem with putting glue or latex on the back of your rug is that it won't stop the loops from pulling out, but it will make them impossible to repair.

Another problem with latex or glue is that it prevents good air circulation. If you wash a rug with latex backing, moisture can't get out, and the backing can rot. Common sense goes a long way: This craft was invented long before latex, and some of those first rugs are still around today.

Explorations in Color

Color is where it all begins. Every individual sees colors differently and uses color in a unique and personal way. Yarn can provide every color effect imaginable for rug hooking, whether you are purchasing colors off the shelf or dyeing yarn for your projects. You can make use of natural colors, or if hand-spinning is an option, you can blend your colors for that "dyed-in-the-wool" effect. Color is the essence of any good design, so let your imagination go when planning your projects.

Sheep and goats come not only in white: They can be naturally gray, brown, black, red, or like my Jacob sheep, spotted black and white. When you make use of natural colors, they never fade or bleed when washed, and they seem to go very well with almost every décor. Natural colors look great on hardwood floors, and really bring out the beauty of wood furniture. Moreover, natural colors can also be overdyed for stunning effects.

Once you have mastered the basic technique for dyeing a solid-colored yarn, you can begin to experiment and modify the process to achieve a great variety of effects. For instance, you can purposely dye your yarn unevenly for primitive rug hooking, or dip-dye yarn for shading realistic flowers, leaves, and scrolls. You can dye yarn for a rich, multi-colored effect, overdye leftovers for harmonious "hit or miss" rugs, or blend colors in the spinning process.

Celtic Interlace Rug, 52" x 48", hand-spun and Halcyon rug yarn in natural colors on linen. Designed and hooked by Judy Taylor, Auburn, Washington, 2001.

Stained Glass Rug, 27" in diameter, overdyed Ewenique 2-ply yarn on linen. Designed and hooked by Judy Taylor, Auburn, Washington, 2001.

Hand-spun yarn being unwound from an umbrella swift to a niddy-noddy and a cross-tied skein, ready for the dye pot.

much yarn is in each skein. Another very useful tool is a "swift" (sometimes called an "umbrella swift" or "skein-winder"), which allows you to wind smaller skeins off a larger skein.

Preparing yarn for the dye pot:
I always tie my skeins in order to keep them from getting tangled in the dyeing process. Using a contrasting yarn, I tie a loose "figure eight" in at least three places on the skein. Then, I loosely tie each of the ends of the skein in a half knot. It is important to tie the skeins loosely so that the dye will be able to soak in evenly.

Cut a 1" sample from the yarn that you are dyeing, so you will be able to test your dye pot before putting in your skeins. In order to get a solid color, the yarn must have plenty of room in the dye pot. I use large canning pots for dyeing, which allow me to dye 1 to $1^1/2$ pounds of yarn evenly.

Many types of dye are available: Some are intended to be used on animal fibers, some on plant fibers. Some dyes are made to be colorfast, and others fade over time. Some dyes come with a mordant mixed in: Others require that you add a mordant. Some dyes come from natural sources, such as flowers, roots, bark, or shells, and can be modified depending on which mordant you choose. Most of the rugs in this book were dyed using Country Classics dyes, which are specifically formulated to be used on animal fibers and have a mordant mixed in the product. Other dyes that work well on wool are Cushing, Ashford, Gaywool, and PRO Chem. (Check out the "Sources" section on page 63 for help finding and choosing your dye products.)

Any utensils used in dyeing, such as

Basic Instructions for Dyeing Yarn a Solid Color

If you have purchased yarn that comes in a ball, you will first need to wind your yarn off the ball into a skein. A "niddy-noddy" is a wooden dowel with bars on either end, set at right angles to each other. This simple tool allows you to wrap your yarn into skeins that are always the same size, which makes it very easy to keep track of how pots, gloves, tongs, measuring spoons, etc., should never be used for cooking afterward.

Dyeing the yarn: To begin dyeing, fill your pot with water about ³/4 full, and bring the water to a slow boil. As soon as the water is beginning to bubble, add your dye in small increments. (You can always add more dye, but it is almost impossible to take dye out if you add too much!) Country Classics dye recommends using 2 teaspoons per 4 ounces of yarn, but I always start with less, and add a little at a time to the dye pot until my sample is the desired color.

A basket of Judy's hand-spun and dyed yarn and a niddy-noddy.

Preparing the dye bath and checking a sample piece.

Drop your sample into the dye pot, and let it sit for a few minutes. If the color is not dark enough, add more dye. If I think I've added all the dye that I should, but I'm still not getting the color dark enough, sometimes a splash of vinegar will give the dye an extra boost. When the sample is the desired color, you can add your skeins to the dye pot.

Hold all of the skeins from one end above the dye pot, and lower all of them in at the same time. Gently push them down so that all parts of the yarn are submerged. Keep in mind that most of the dye will be absorbed in the first 10 minutes, so make sure that your skeins can move around in the pot. If neces-

Lowering skeins into the dye bath.

Yarn dyed a solid color in my dye pot (note that I use a large canning pot for dyeing), with a rinsed, dyed skein and the original color alongside the dye bath.

Rinsing the dyed yarn.

A multi-colored skein, two-toned yarn in skein, two-toned yarn in a ball, and a ball winder with the original color of the yarn.

sary, gently raise and lower the skeins to assure even dyeing for the first 10 minutes, then let the yarn simmer for 20 more minutes.

Rinsing the yarn: After the yarn has simmered for 20 minutes, I transfer my dye pot to one side of the sink and fill a clean pot with hot water on the other side. **It is important never to shock your yarn from hot to cold when it is wet, as this will cause the wool fibers to felt.** When the rinse pot is filled with hot water, I add a splash of dishwashing liquid.

Wear rubber gloves and use tongs to raise one skein at a time out of the dye pot and transfer it to the rinse pot. When all of the skeins have been taken out of the dye pot, pour out the dye and rinse the dye pot. Then fill it with hot water just as you did in the first rinse pot, only don't add soap this time.

The yarn gradually cools off while it is going through the rinsing process, and soon you should be able to lift it and squeeze it with your **gloved** hands. Just squeeze the skein in your hands. Never twist or wring it out, as this too can cause the wool fibers to felt. I transfer the yarn from one rinse pot to the next until the water runs clear when the yarn is squeezed. Empty out all of the rinse water, and squeeze as much water from the skeins as you can.

"Wuzzing the wool": The next step is what the old-timers called "wuzzing the wool." I take the yarn outside for this step, and gripping one end of a skein, I swing the skein hard in a circle several times, which removes a good deal of the remaining water. Then I hang the skeins to dry. On a hot, sunny day, the yarn will dry in a day; indoors, it may take a couple of days for the yarn to dry thoroughly. Once the yarn is dry, remove the cross-ties, and twist one end of the skein four or five times, fold it over, and tuck one end inside the other.

Getting ready to hook: As soon as the yarn is needed for rug hooking, it should be wound off into a center-pull ball. Tuck one end of the skein over your thumb, and start wrapping the yarn around your fingers. (A swift is very handy for this step, but you can also have a companion hold the skein while you unwind it.) When you are nearing the end of the skein, slip the ball off your fingers, and start wrapping the rest of the yarn around the outside of the ball, making sure you don't lose track of the center end. Tuck the outside end under, and when you hook, pull from the center end. You can also purchase a ball winder, which makes even, professional looking balls.

Tess Rug, 27" x 17¹/₂", hand-spun wool on linen. Designed and hooked by Judy Taylor, Auburn, Washington, 1998.

Definitions in Color

Mordant: A chemical applied to wool to open up fibers, so they will accept dye. If you looked at a wool fiber under a microscope, you would see that it is covered with scales, layered like the shingles on a roof. In order to make the dye adhere to the fiber, those scales have to be opened up, so the dye can get into the center of the fiber. Some examples of mordants are cream of tartar, vinegar, alum, iron, lime, copper, and uric acid. Different mordants can produce different colors with the same dye.

Felting: A physical change in the wool, in which the scaly fibers permanently mesh together. Wool can be felted when it is shocked from hot to cold while it is wet or by agitating the wool when it is wet. Felting is a necessary process used to create the fabric strips for traditional rug hooking. If the woven fabric were not felted, it would fall apart when cut into thin strips for rug hooking. Felting, however, is not recommended when working with yarn. Yarn is strong, durable, and balanced, and does not need felting in order to be held together. Indeed, felting the yarn would cause it to stick together, and would compact the loft out of the yarn.

Primitive Rugs

Welcome Friend, rug with yarn samples, 33" x 22",   Ewenique 2-ply yarn, overdyed for a mottled effect, on linen. Designed and hooked by Judy Taylor, Auburn, Washington, 2002.

Primitive rug hooking is a modern craft inspired by rugs produced in the late 1700s and 1800s before the Industrial Revolution hit North America. I actually find the term "primitive" to be misleading, since it implies simple or easy. The craft is imitative of the work of the pioneers. Not only are we attempting to recreate the style of rugs that early Americans produced, but we are also attempting to create the look of age. Much thought and planning goes into hooking primitives, but a well-planned project is a joy to hook and a work of art to appreciate.

A Glimpse Back in Time

The primitive rugs that we find so charming today were created out of necessity. Our pioneer farmwife (let's call her Sarah, to make the story easier to tell) had little leisure time between milking the cow, washing the clothes, scaring off hungry bears, and baking her daily bread. Her rug making was not a pastime craft activity; it was rooted in practicality. She made rugs because she needed them.

She used raw materials that were already on hand, such as used feed sacks for backing, recycled woolen fabric, yarn that she spun herself from her own sheep, and natural dyes that she gathered from her area. Her choice of yarn or fabric strips for hooking would have been determined by what she had on hand. When Pa's wool trousers became too worn to be respectable, they would not be thrown away, but cut up and reused in her next project. Wool yarn was a renewable resource, which she could produce as needed. Her rugs would likely have been made with a mixture of both yarn and fabric.

Sarah would have found rug hooking to be an ideal form of rug making because the only tool needed, other than scissors, was a hand-held hook. She could easily justify packing a simple hook in the covered wagon for the next big move. Rug hooking served a very useful purpose, steeped in practicality, and thus became a very popular craft in the pioneer household.

But rug hooking was popular for more than just practical reasons. If all Sarah needed was a plain old rug, she could have thrown two pounds of yarn into a pot and hooked a one-color rug. Sarah could not resist the idea of a blank canvas. She had a wealth of creative ideas to express, and rug hooking gave her the medium.

When you think about it, Sarah was a pretty gutsy lady. She very likely left behind all of her family and friends and ventured with her husband into an untamed wilderness to build a home and raise a family. Every creature comfort was made from scratch. The daily challenges in her life required her to summon up all her strength to provide for her family. She had to be courageous. She had to be a problem-solver. By definition, Sarah was a very creative person.

Primitives appeal to us today because they mirror the ideas of the unique person who made them. William Winthrop Kent in his book, *The Hooked Rug*, wrote that the value of a hooked rug depended in a large part on the design. "They tell a story. Their personal qualities appeal to us because subconsciously, we feel that some interesting or ambitious human being is trying to express him or herself in every design." Sarah simply could not pass up the opportunity to express her creative ideas, so she poured them into her hooked rugs.

Her subjects were familiar to her: the family dog, the cabin, flowers, trees, and the wildlife all around her. She also borrowed from the quiltmaking craft, using geometrics in her designs. Her style was impressionistic. She had much more in common with Monet than Michelangelo (although she probably never heard of either one!). A flower did not have to look realistic. Size, color, and proportion were whimsical. It was the idea of a flower that she was

going for, not realism.

Primitives were crudely drawn, and as such, they rarely contained straight lines or right angles. Designs may lack proportion (the dog and the house may

PHOTOGRAPH COURTESY OF LES RUPP

Rebecca Landin hooking during Traditional Rug Hooking Week at Sauder Village in Archbold, Ohio.

Left: The "right" way to dye yarn. In this pot the yarn is floating loosely with plenty of room to move around.

Right: The primitive way to dye. The yarn is crammed together to create a variegated color effect.

be the same size, for example.) Most design elements were outlined, sometimes with odd colors. In my *Welcome Friend* rug, I outlined the black horse with gold to make it stand out against the background. (See page 28.)

Since Sarah was working with natural dyes, her palette was limited to the colors available, but they usually included yellows, greens, browns, reds, and some blues. The results of her dye pot were usually uneven, so her projects had a textured, mottled quality. Natural dyes fade over time. Sarah may have been able to produce bright colors in her dye pot, but they would mellow over the years.

Creating Primitives Today

When we create primitive rugs today, we are trying to imitate the effects of age on new materials. The best way I've found to recreate these warm, faded colors is to begin with a light-colored yarn, such as light brown or gray. Two of my favorite Country Classics colors for primitive projects are Maize and Pumpkin. If I dyed a white yarn with these colors, I would end up with a bright and brassy yellow and orange. But when I overdye a natural-colored yarn, the Maize gives me a light yellow-green, and the Pumpkin provides shades of gold. Experiment with overdyeing light colored yarns or fabric to achieve those warm, antique tones.

The real hallmark of a primitive rug is the variegation in the yarn (or fabric). Throw out everything you learned in Chapter 5 about the "right" way to dye yarn. First of all, to get the mottled effect that I'm looking for, I use less water in the dye bath and cram the yarn down so that some parts of the yarn soak up more dye than other spots. You could also sprinkle a little extra dye on the top of the dye bath when all the yarn is wet. Or try to sprinkle a slightly different color on top. Don't allow the yarn to move around in the dye pot while it is simmering.

Then, when you hook with these variegated yarns, follow the contours of the shapes in continuous rows, so that as the yarn changes colors, the design elements are echoed (see the illustration on page 31). It is this pleasing richness in texture in the background and design elements that we enjoy in primitive rugs. Getting the variegation right in the yarn is the key to successful primitives. With the right yarn, the rugs practically hook themselves! (See page 62 for complete instructions on hooking a primitive pillow.)

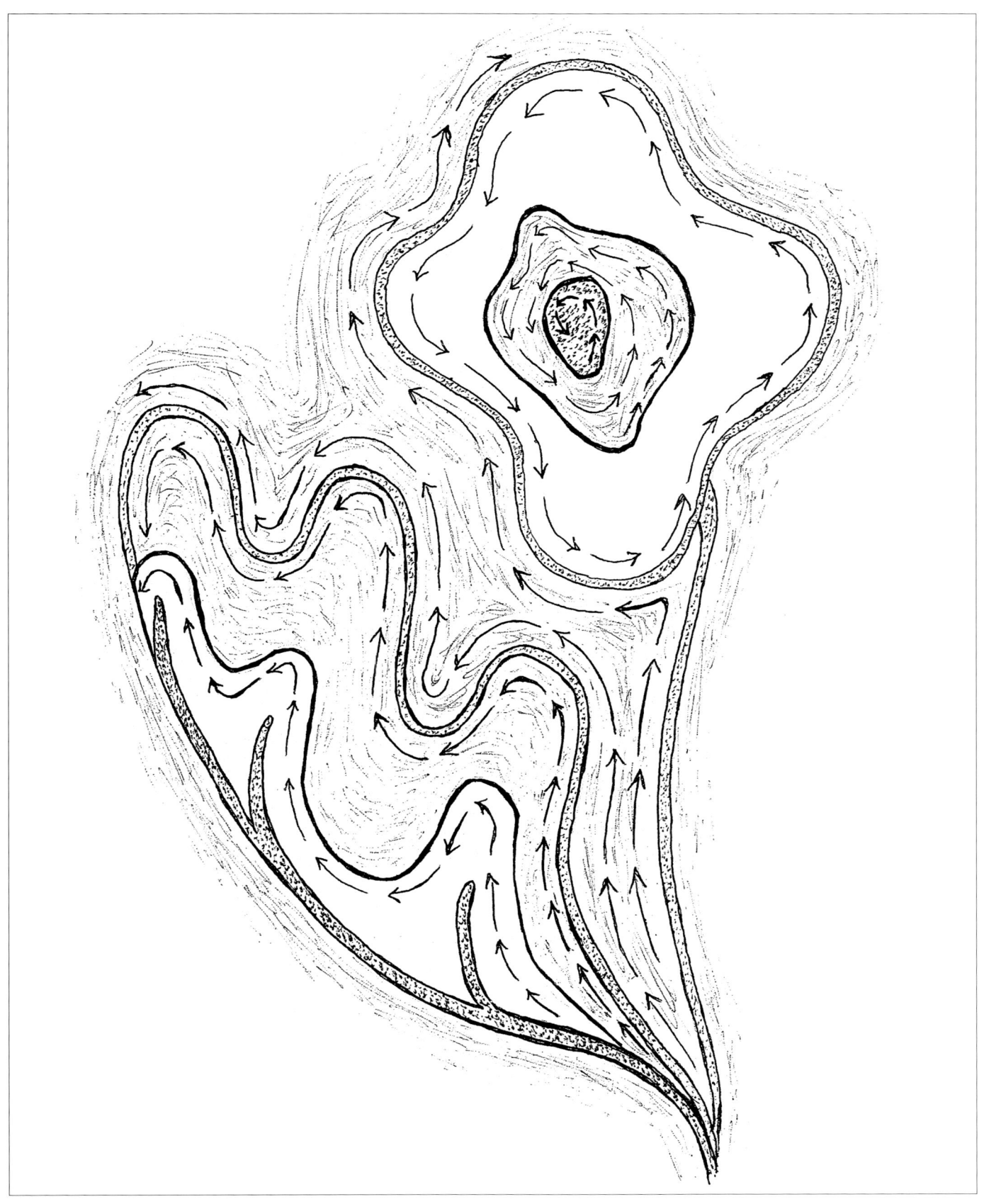

The primitive rug hooking technique.

Dyeing Yarn for Shading
Flowers, Leaves, and Scrolls

Antique Flower Rug, 33¹/₂" x 24¹/₂", dip-dyed and hand-spun yarn and New Zealand Wool Pak yarn on linen. Designed and hooked by Judy Taylor, Auburn, Washington, 2002.

Preparing Yarn for Dip Dyeing

For most flowers and scrolls, I like to work with 6" strands of dip-dyed yarn. This gives me some variety of colors to work with on each strand, while maintaining the gradation of color from dark to light. Then, when I hook, I create the shading effect with the yarn itself. I start hooking the inside of a rose petal, for

An assortment of the yarn used to hook my **Antique Flower Rug.**

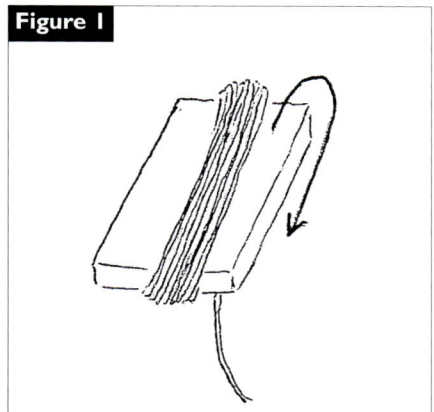

Figure 1

example, using the dark end of the strand, and then I hook outward. That way, the yarn itself fades in color as I hook, making it seem like the petal is brighter on the outside. For a rose 3" to 4" in diameter, I like to have on hand approximately 160 - 6" strands.

1. To get my 6" strands, I start by wrapping yarn around a 6" form—a paperback book or a piece of cardboard—a few dozen times, thereby creating a small hank of yarn for dip-dyeing. For the rose I would first wrap

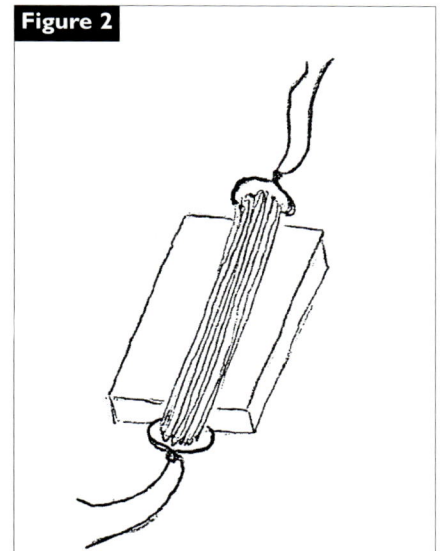

Figure 2

around the paperback book 40 times, then I would create another hank in the same way (for a total of 80 - 12" wraps). When the hanks have been dyed and dried, I will be cutting both ends of the

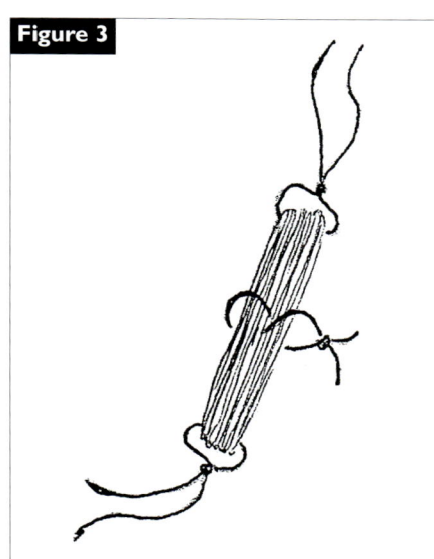

Figure 3

hank, so I will end up with 160 - 6" strands.

2. Before removing a hank from the paperback book, I tie both ends with a contrasting colored yarn, leaving 3 to 4

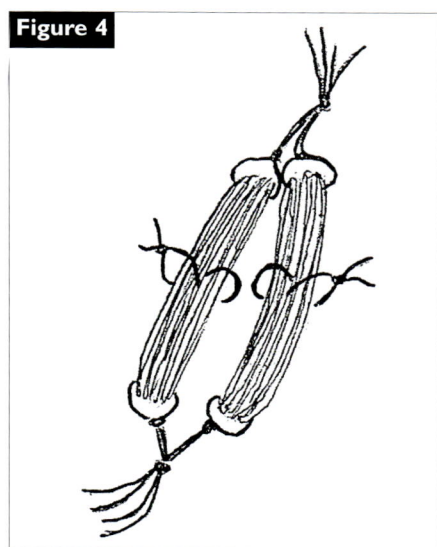

Figure 4

extra inches of contrast yarn for later use.

3. Then I slip the hank off the book, and tie it in the middle in a figure eight (this keeps the strands organized, so they won't get bunched up or tangled in the dyeing process).

4. I then tie a knot in the extra contrast yarn on the ends, so I have something to hold on to and can weigh them down in the dye pot if needed. If I plan to dye more than one hank in the same jar, I tie all the tops together and all the bottoms together.

Preparing the Dye Pot

Put about 2" of water into jars (you can use mason jars, mayonnaise jars, etc.). Add water to the dye pot to a level of about 2" of water. Plan to have enough jars for the number of hanks being dyed, plus one extra jar per color (2 to 4 hanks can be dyed at the same time in a mayonnaise or mason jar). The extra jar is for a slightly weaker dye solution that you may need to add to the jars with yarn in them.

When the water comes to a boil, add a very small amount of dye to each of the jars (I start with about $1/8$ of a teaspoon). You can always add more dye to the jar if the yarn is not coming out dark enough, but it is impossible to remove dye from the yarn if you start out with too much color.

Testing the Color

Drop a 1" sample of the yarn you wish to dye into each of the jars, to test for color. Leave the samples in for a few minutes; then take them out and rinse them. The color you are trying for is the darkest shade that you want on your strands. If the sample color is too dark, pour out a little dye in the sink, and replace with water. If the color is not dark enough, add a little more dye. Test that jar with another 1" sample until you have achieved the color you want on the darkest end of

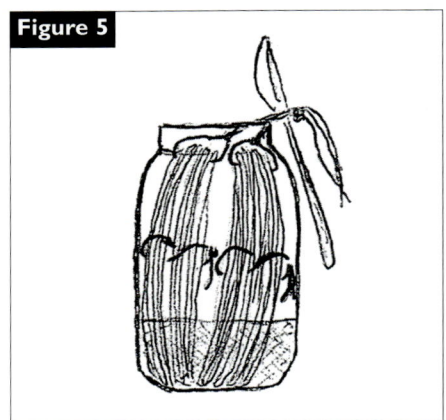

Figure 5

your strand.

Begin Dyeing

1. Lower the hanks of yarn into the dye jars, so the first 2" of the hanks sit in the dye bath. If you need something to hold

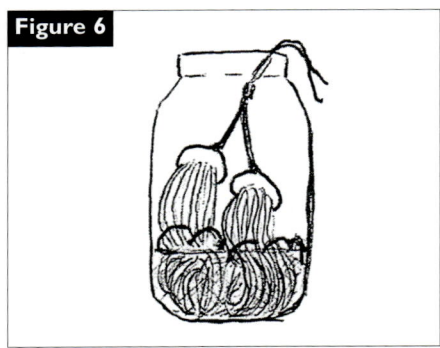

Figure 6

up the hanks so they will stay in this position, a spoon makes a good weight.
2. Let the hanks sit in this spot for about 3 to 4 minutes, then begin to gently dip them down into the dye bath. Keep raising and dipping the hanks until you have some faded dye all the way up to the top of the hank.

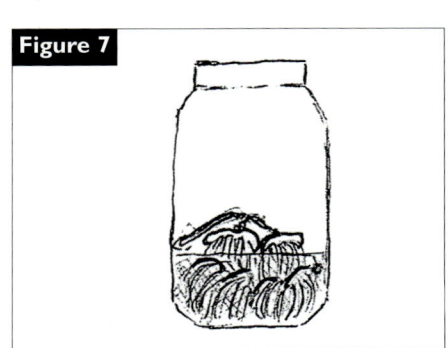

Figure 7

Dip-dyeing yarn in jars.

3. Sometimes the yarn absorbs the dye very quickly, so that the dye bath is nearly exhausted when you begin to dip the hanks. If this happens, lift the hank up out of the dye bath, and with a syringe, infuse some of the weaker dye solution from the extra jar into the upper portions of the hank, so that you have a medium strength color in the middle, fading up to the top.

4. When the hank is the desired color, let it rest in the jar (push it down so it is covered in water), and continue simmering for about 20 more minutes. You can check the hank periodically to make sure the color is setting the way you want it.

5. If you are satisfied with the gradation of color from dark to light on your hank, but you don't feel that the bottom came out dark enough, you can lift the hank out of the dye bath. Then add more dye (never add dye directly to the yarn, add it to the dye bath, stir, and then dip the hank). Dip the hank into the darker dye a few times, so that you don't end up with an abrupt difference between dark and light. When the hank is the desired color, let it simmer for another 20 minutes, checking occasionally to make sure the color is setting the way you want.

Dip-dyed hanks, cut on both ends, drying on a towel and dip-dyed samples in a fabric holder.

Figure 8

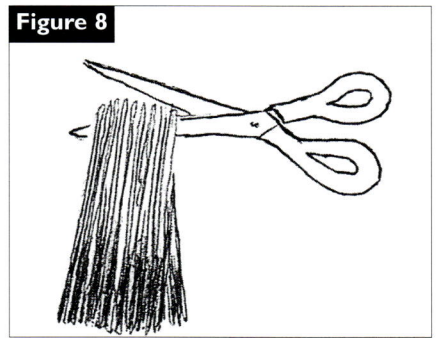

Figure 9

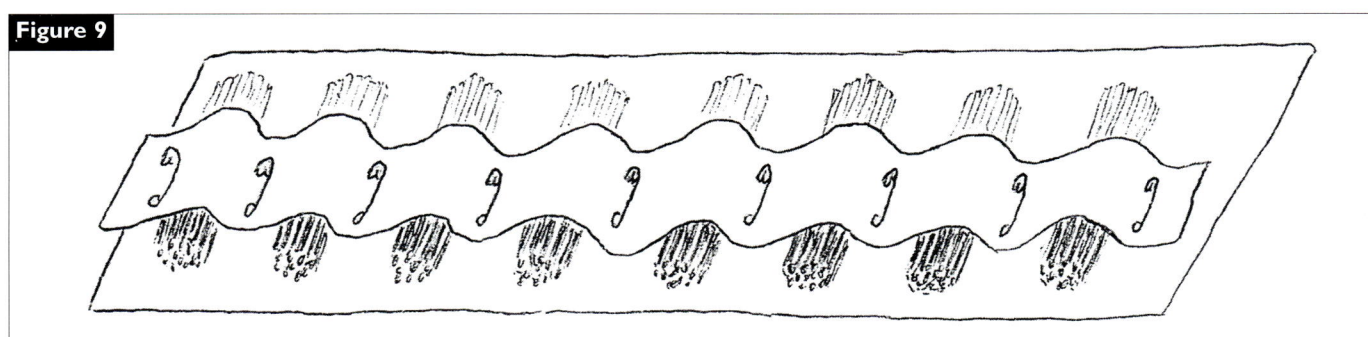

Judy's fabric carrier for her dip-dyed yarns.

Rinsing the Yarn

When the dyeing is done, rinse the hanks in hot water (see rinsing instructions in Chapter 5), and hang to dry. If you wish to hasten the drying time, you can cut both ends of the hank, remove the figure eight tie from the middle, and carefully spread the strands out on a towel or screen to dry.

Keeping Your Dip-Dyed Yarn Organized for Storage

If you have dyed many colors for your project, you can keep the colors organized in a simple fabric holder. For the bottom part, cut a 6" x 24" piece of fabric (cotton works well), and make the top piece 3" x 36". Center the top piece on the end of the bottom piece, and pin into place. Then place your first color on the bottom, and bring the top piece over the yarn. Pin the top to the bottom and put the next color on the bottom, and pin the top down over the yarn. Continue until all of your colors have their own little slot in the fabric carrier. When you want to put your rug project away, you can simply roll up the fabric, and all of your yarn will stay organized and untangled. Your fabric holder can be re-used as needed for future projects. (See page 57 for complete instructions for hooking a shaded rose with dip-dyed yarn.)

Other Color Effects: Blending Multi-Colored Yarn and Overdyeing

Jacob Farm Rug, 36" x 25", hand-spun and blended yarn, mohair, and wool fabric strips on linen. Designed and hooked by Judy Taylor, Auburn, Washington, 1998.

In my years of hooking with yarn, I have found that yarn is a more versatile artistic medium than most people think. I have found nothing that can be done with fabric strips that cannot also be done with yarn. In fact, a few effects that can be achieved with yarn are just not possible with fabric strips.

The Advantages of Hand-Spinning

Hand-spinning allows a rug maker the unique chance to design yarn from scratch. Dyed or natural-colored wools can be blended for a "dyed-in-the-wool" effect, which cannot be done by dyeing yarn or fabric. Blended colors can be quite subtle, and they can

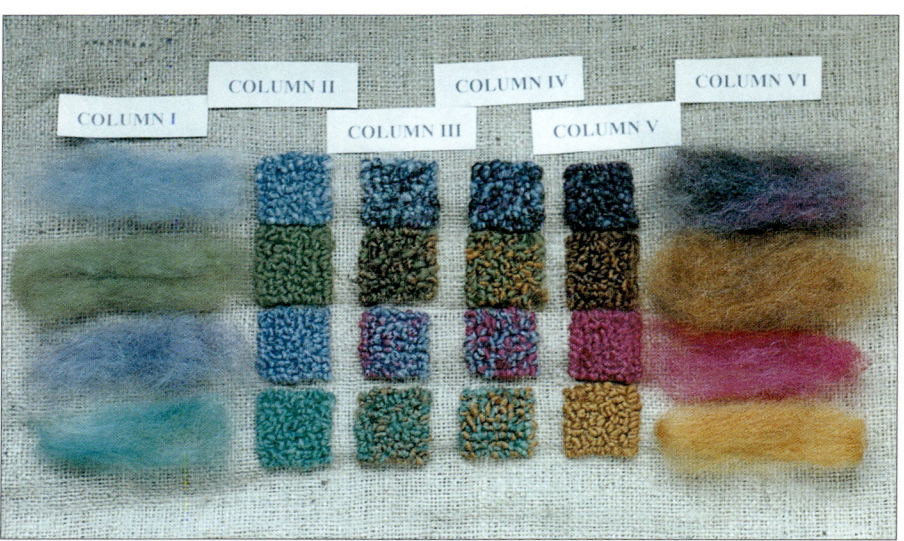

Blending colors in the spinning process: Column 1: Wool Sample A. Column II: Sample A spun into a two-ply yarn. Column III: Sample A blended with Sample B: Column IV: A single strand of A plied with a single strand of B. Column V: Sample B spun into a two-ply yarn. Column VI: Wool Sample B.

add an extra depth and mystery to a rug. The heathered effect of a blended color is unique. These blended colors can be used by themselves for a beautiful effect or designed to create shading and perspective.

All of the yarn in my *Jacob Farm* rug was hand-spun, but none of the yarn was dyed for the project. All of the colors you see in the rug were in the wool before I began. The wool was either natural-colored or dyed, but then the colors were blended or plied together to achieve a wide variety of effects.

Painting with Yarn

The yarn for the grass in my *Jacob Farm* rug, for example, was blended to give the effect of perspective. In the foreground, I blended avocado and spring green wool, and then I threw in a lock of dyed mohair every once in a while to make it look like tiny flowers were growing under the sheep's feet.

As the field extended back toward the buildings, I blended avocado with brown, increasing the brown and decreasing the avocado the further back I went. I also spun single plies of avocado and brown and plied them together so that I would get dots of color occasionally.

The mohair factor: The other advantage of blending is that I can mix fibers for interesting effects. Mohair is a strong, lustrous fiber that takes dye readily. Mohair not only adds strength and durability to my rug yarn, but it also allows me to achieve interesting

Roses and Diamonds, 27" x 21", Ewenique and New Zealand Wool Pak on linen. Designed and hooked by Judy Taylor, Auburn, Washington, 2001.

effects in the dye pot. For example, if I blend white mohair with gray wool, the result will be a soft gray color. When I dye that yarn, however, I can get a greater range of colors than I could with 100% wool because the mohair takes the dye more deeply. The added luster of mohair makes my yarn truly unique.

I also incorporated fabric strips in the *Jacob Farm* rug. I found that an old gray wool blanket gave me the appearance of shingles in the roof of the house. (For more information on using yarn and fabric strips together in the same rug, see the sidebar on page 42.)

Multi-Colored Yarn

Sometimes I will intentionally dye yarn two different colors. For instance, I might wish to jazz up a background yarn for a more interesting effect. I primarily use two methods to get these multi-colored effects: One is to mix colors in the same dye pot, and the other is to move the yarn from one dye pot to another.

Layering colors in the same dye pot: In the first method, I will prepare my dye pot with one color, say Country Classics Desert Rose. I will then cram my yarn down into the rose dye, until it is submerged but doesn't have room to move around. Then I could sprinkle Persimmon or some other color on the top, and poke down on the yarn a bit so that the second color mixes a bit with the yarn on top. The top color will be slightly different from the color on the bottom of the dye pot. Don't let the yarn move around in the dye process, so that the yarn takes color differently from top to bottom. The results from this method are always totally unique,

Dyeing in balls for a two-toned effect.

Layering colors in the same dye pot. (Yarn is in a Slate Blue dye bath with Evergreen sprinkled on top.)

sometimes even surprising. No two dye baths will ever be the same, and the yarn you create will be one of a kind.

Dyeing in balls for a two-toned effect: Mixing dyes in the same dye pot produces a blended effect, but you can

39

A multi-colored basket of yarn.

The same yarn overdyed with Country Classics Ripe Tomato, Kiwi, and Pumpkin. (This yarn was then used in the *Crown of Thorns* rug on page 41.)

also dye yarn in different colors with very little overlap. The best way to get a truly two-colored effect is if you have a ball-winder, which creates regularly sized balls with flat bottoms. The flat bottom is crucial, as it allows the ball to sit evenly in the dye bath.

I add water to two dye pots, so that they are both about 2" deep. When the water comes to a boil, I add a dye color to the first dye pot. I then set the balls in the dye, so they are halfway submerged. I let them sit until they have simmered for 20 minutes. Then, I add a different dye to the second dye pot. I turn the balls over, and let them sit half-submerged in the second dye bath for 20 more minutes.

After the balls have simmered in the second dye bath for 20 minutes, they can be rinsed out. The best way to rinse them is to fill a pot with clean, hot water, add a splash of dishwashing liquid, and set the balls into the rinse pot. Gently squeeze each ball (make sure you have gloves on), and transfer them to another rinse pot filled with hot water, but no soap. Keep transferring the yarn from one rinse pot to another until the water runs clear. Wind the wet, rinsed yarn into a skein, and hang to dry.

Overdyeing Different Colors

Overdyeing, whether you are dyeing natural colors or previously dyed wool, can produce dazzling effects. Any yarn that you see on the shelf at a yarn store, or the scraps of leftovers from previous projects, can be overdyed.

Once you get used to the idea, you will never look at color in the same way. You may have some yarn that is boring in color, but that is just the color it is now! With a dye pot and a little imagination, it can be transformed from bland to amazing.

My *Crown of Thorns* rug is a perfect example of the delightful effects of overdyeing. Like many traditional quilt patterns, the *Crown of Thorns* design lends itself to "hit or miss" colors. (For more information on "hit or miss" rugs, see Chapter Nine on page 43.) The first time I made this rug, I just raided my scrap bags using bright colors, dull colors, and everything I could find. The effect was cheerful and bright. But when that rug sold, I faced a dilemma. I loved the pattern, but I hated the idea of making another rug exactly like the first.

Then I read about a rug maker named Martha Morris in the June/July/August 2002 issue of *Rug Hooking*. According to the article, Martha hooked all of her 70 rugs using only three dye colors. The rug featured in the magazine seemed very colorful, but the colors were harmonized because, while she only used three dye colors, she overdyed many different colors to achieve this unique result.

I couldn't resist giving Martha's method a try, and *Crown of Thorns* seemed like the perfect project. I took the same scrap bags of all sorts of color that I used in my first *Crown of Thorns* rug, and I threw them into three dye-pots, using Country Classics Ripe Tomato, Kiwi, and Pumpkin. The effect is still very much "hit or miss," but the colors look like they belong together.

One note about hooking "hit or miss" rugs: Hooking with little bits of odd col-

Crown of Thorns (a "hit or miss" rug), 36" x 22", overdyed yarn on linen. Designed and hooked by Judy Taylor, Auburn, Washington, 2002.

ors can be very liberating, like coloring with crayons. There are no rules, just color play. You don't want your project to be so busy, however, that you can't make out the design. In the *Crown of Thorns* rug, I decided to make the background of each crown section out of the same two colors, and I gave the "window panes" the same color treatment. This really made the crowns stand out.

Crown of Thorns (a "hit or miss" rug), 36" x 22", brightly colored yarn on linen. Designed and hooked by Judy Taylor, Auburn, Washington, 2000.

Yarn and Fabric Strips:
A Match Made in Heaven

In his book, *The Hooked Rug*, William Winthrop Kent shows evidence that hooked rugs were probably first made by Yorkshire weavers in the 1600s as a way to use up "thrums," or extra bits of leftover yarn. He also points to historical evidence that sailors took up the craft because it helped seamen pass the time on long voyages, without taking up too much space on the crowded vessels. He makes reference to rugs being made at the time by weavers and sailors using both yarn and cut strips of fabric. Although he offers no explanation as to why the rug makers began to use fabric strips, it is clear in his study that the craft was entirely practical in nature. If leftover yarn could be put to use in rug making, why not leftover fabric as well?

Like the British sailors and weavers, I am a great fan of making use of what you have. My love for yarn and hand-spinning led me to rug hooking as a way to use up my yarn. But wool fabric is also available in abundance and can make wonderful rugs.

I find fabric strips to be very useful when I need straight lines or a geometric effect. In my *Jacob Farm* rug, for example, I cut up strips from a wool blanket and hooked the strips in the roof of the farmhouse and barn. The loops of the fabric strips appear rectangular, unlike yarn, so the material itself gave the impression of shingles on the roof, without any other design effort on my part. If I had used yarn hooking the roof, I would have had to find some other way of representing shingles.

Fabric can also be used to create contrast in detail areas. I am often surprised that two skeins of yarn that seem to contrast when I look at them side by side sometimes blend together when hooked side by side. If I hook a row of fabric strips between the two colors, dyed the same color as one of the skeins, I can create contrast with texture without bringing in another color.

Aurora Borealis, 46" x 29½", "hit or miss" yarn on linen. Designed and hooked by Judy Taylor, Auburn, Washington, 1995.

Fabric strips make an excellent addition to primitive rugs. If you are dyeing variegated yarn for background and design areas, include swatches of wool fabric in your dye pot. Then, when you hook, you can alternate between yarn and fabric in the same area, adding texture and visual interest to your rug. Of course, fabric strips can easily be incorporated in any "hit or miss" design.

Wool fabric can be dyed just like yarn, using the same process and dyes that are covered in Chapters 5 through 8 of this book. The fabric should only be dyed in large pieces before they are cut into strips. If you tried to put cut strips through the dyeing and rinsing process, I am afraid you would end up with a frayed mess. Once the fabric is cut into strips, that is the color it will remain. So if you have leftover strips of wool fabric from a rug project, just bag them up and store them with your "hit or miss" bags. No doubt a project will come along for which those colors will be perfect.

A detail of the house on Judy's **Jacob Farm** rug that shows wool fabric strips and yarn blended seamlessly together.

Leftover Yarns from Old Projects

Teapot Rug, 29" x 19", "hit or miss" and wool yarn on linen. Designed and hooked by Judy Taylor, Auburn, Washington, 1998.

Many people involved in other yarn crafts are also attracted to rug hooking as a fun way to use up leftover yarns from knitting, crochet, or weaving projects. Indeed, it seems that no matter how many "hit or miss" rugs I make, my leftover bags never seem to get any smaller!

"Hit or Miss" Rugs

Nothing ever goes to waste in rug hooking. Scraps of yarn can be hooked using a "hit or miss" technique. Much like a patchwork quilt, rug hookers can create very interesting and colorful effects by hooking with small amounts of many colors in stripes, geometrics, waves, lines, polka dots, abstracts, etc. Small areas of the rug can be "hit or miss," such as a border or background. Or entire rug designs

can be done in "hit or miss," such as in quilt designs (see two versions of the *Crown of Thorns* rug on page 41).

One thing to keep in mind if an entire rug is going to be "hit or miss" is to designate at least one feature to be the same throughout so the rug doesn't appear too busy. I usually choose an outline and a common element such as the squares in my *Log Cabin Rug* to be the repeated colors. The background in my *Penny Rug* is dark, so the pennies show up in contrast. If a penny was too dark to show up against my background color, I would outline it for better contrast.

Another "hit or miss" technique is using small amounts of leftovers to hook smaller detail areas in a rug, such as flowers, leaves, or any other area where you just need a spot of color. In my *Teapot Rug*, the teapots, outlines, and lettering were all hooked with leftover yarns from other projects, and the border and background yarns were selected to pull the design together.

"Hit or miss" can also be used in especially high traffic areas on a rug, so worn areas can be easily replaced. On stair runners, for example, the part of the step facing you when you are walking up the stairs can be decorated much like a wallhanging, using whatever yarn is appropriate for the picture. The landing of the step, particularly the middle of the step, however, can be done in a "hit or miss" pattern. That way, if the landing gets worn out over time, it is no trouble at all replacing the yarn because anything will work! You

Penny Rug, 27" x 40", wool and alpaca yarn on linen. Designed and hooked by Judy Taylor, Auburn, Washington, 1996.

hooked. I either make my loops closer together when hooking with lighter weight yarns, or I double the yarn while hooking by drawing both ends of the ball up and hooking two strands in each loop.

When hooking with yarns of different weight, keep in mind that all of your loops need to be the same height. Otherwise, the thick yarn will spread out and swallow up the finer yarn!

Sometimes, odd colors end up in your "hit or miss" bags, such as a brassy green or a blah beige. As you read in Chapter 8, even the weirdest, dullest, or brassiest colors can be overdyed for stunning effect. I store my leftovers in clear plastic bags, organized by color, so that I can easily find the right yarns for my project.

Traveling Rugs

"Hit or miss" rugs make great traveling projects. Twice, on trips to Europe that I took with my family, I hooked a traveling rug, using yarn that we gathered on our trip. I simply brought the pattern on linen and carried a hook in my suitcase, and just like a treasure hunt, we sought out spinners and yarn stores wherever we could. I worked on the rug in the evenings on our trip and shared the craft with people everywhere we went.

In 1996, we traveled through England, Ireland, Scotland, and Norway. I needed a project that was large enough to keep me busy in the evenings, but we were also determined to travel light. To avoid carrying several pounds of yarn around, I decided on the *Penny Rug* design. That way, we could gather small samples, a little at a time, and I could hook a few pennies each

don't have to worry about matching colors or making your repair "invisible." If it is "hit or miss," the repair won't show up anyway.

Often yarns that are used in other crafts, such as knitting and weaving, are thinner than the typical rug hooking yarn. This doesn't mean they cannot be evening. When it came time for me to decide on a background yarn, we found a hand-spinner in Ireland (not an easy task, as we were told, "they're thin on the ground!") who sold me a beautiful hand-spun alpaca yarn. Alpaca is a soft fiber. It is not the most durable yarn for rug hooking, but finding this hand-spun treasure was not something that I was willing to pass up. I doubled the yarn as I hooked (hooking two strands at a time). The rug is now kept in a gentle traffic area by our bed.

In 2000, the family again traveled to Europe, this time visiting France, Switzerland, Germany, Norway, and the British Isles. The *Log Cabin* design worked very well for me on that trip because I would work continuously on one color at a time, repeating the pattern in each square from one end of the rug to the other before I would need another skein. We noticed on this trip that the yarns that we could find were lighter weight knitting and weaving yarns. I either hooked my loops closer together, or I doubled the yarn while I hooked. The overall effect of using the lighter weight yarns is that the rug has a finer look to it. The colors really jump out at you, despite the fact that the lines are so thin.

These two traveling rugs were fun to make, and they were a great conversation starter on our trip. But I treasure them because they are the best kind of souvenirs possible. We have many memories attached to where the yarn came from, friends we met, and experiences we had. We are planning another trip to Europe for next summer, and I am already designing my new traveling rug project!

Log Cabin Rug, 45" x 26", wool yarn on linen. Designed and hooked by Judy Taylor, Auburn, Washington, 2000.

Finishing Your Rug

O nce you have finished hooking your rug, trim away any extra backing, leaving about 4" all around for a hem. You could simply fold the backing under and do a simple hem, but that is not the best way to hem a floor rug because the folded edge can become compressed over time, and the fibers can begin to break, unraveling some of the hooked edges of your rug.

Binding the Edge

A better method of finishing your rug is to bind the edge.

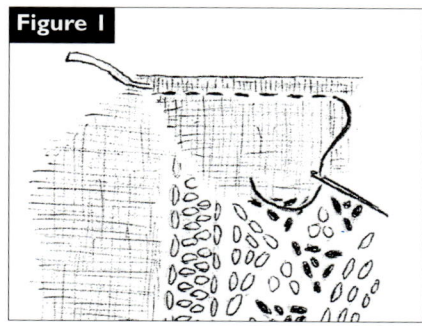

Figure 1

1. Wrap your extra linen around 3/16" cotton cording, and tack the cording in place, close to the hooked edge of the rug.

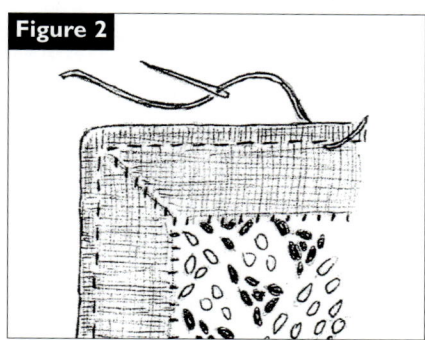

Figure 2

2. Then with matching yarn and a tapestry needle, whipstitch the edge. I begin with my needle going back to

front, but I don't tie a knot with the binding yarn.

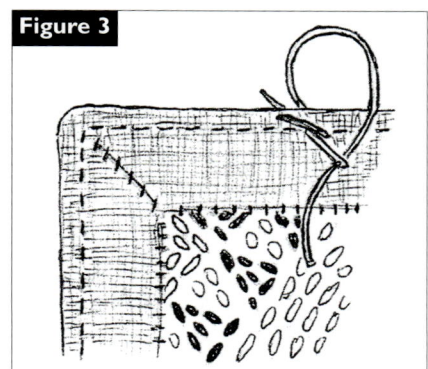

Figure 3

3. I leave about 1" sticking out in the back. Then as I whipstitch, I simply sew over the end.

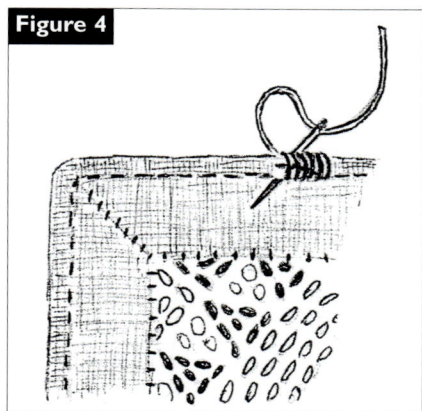

Figure 4

4. I start the section with the needle going back to front, but after the first few stitches, I turn the needle around, so that for the next section, until I run out of yarn on the needle, I am stitching front to back.

5. When I come to the end of the yarn on the needle, I pull the end out to the back, start a new needle, and come in, back to front again. Now I have two ends in the back, and I continue to whipstitch, sewing over both ends.

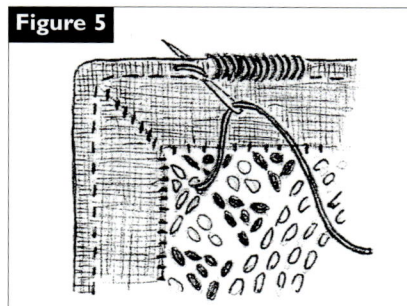

Figure 5

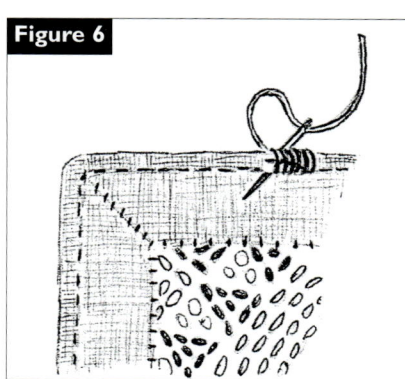

Figure 6

6. Again, at some point I change directions so that my needle is going front to back, so the next end will be in the back.

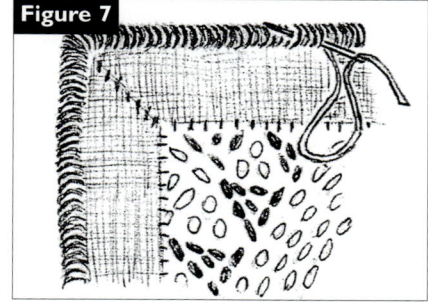

Figure 7

7. When I have whipstitched the whole edge, I sew the last of the yarn under about 1" of the first whipstitches, and cut it off, so that the final end is sewn over as well.

Hemming the Rug

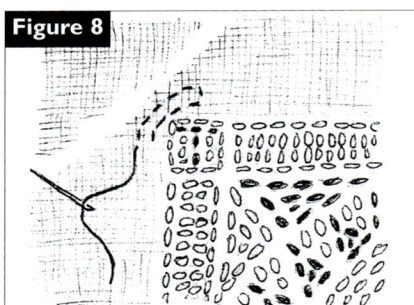

Figure 8

1. Turn the rest of the linen backing under for a hem, and pin into place. If your rug has square corners, you can trim away a little of the excess, and miter the corners. Make sure that you leave at least 1" from the hooked corner uncut, so that if you should ever have to take the rug apart and do some repair, there will still be some linen left intact on the corners. However, you can trim away a triangle of fabric on the corners, which reduces the bulk in your hem.

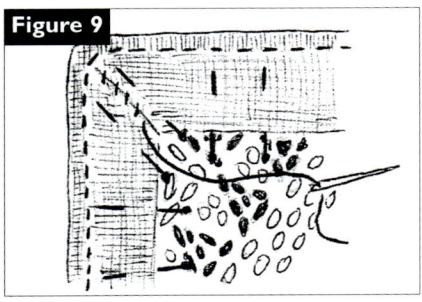

Figure 9

2. It is a good idea to hem your rug with upholstery thread. Be sure you take deep stitches, so that you are stitching the backing of your rug, not sewing the hem to yarn. Dig down deep for your hemstitches. If you are sewing your hem to yarn, you will just end up pulling out loops. I don't even try to make my hem invisible. If ever I should have to take this rug apart, I don't want to have to dig around looking for the stitches.

Note: You can hem the rug immediately after you wrap the cotton cording and tack it in place (see Step 1 in "Binding the Edge"), but I prefer this method. This way, if your backing bunches up at all while you are binding the edge, you will have an easy time fixing the backing before you hem it.

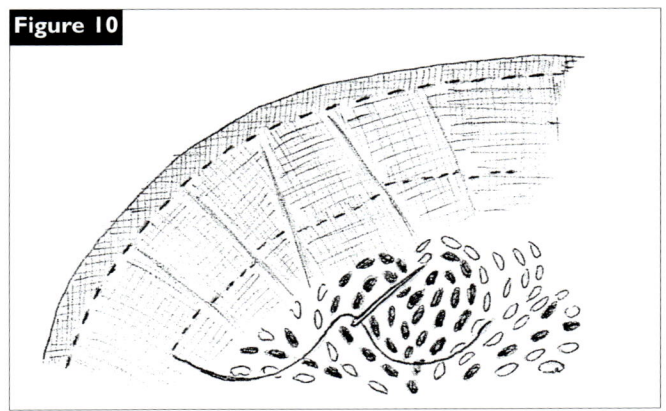

Figure 10

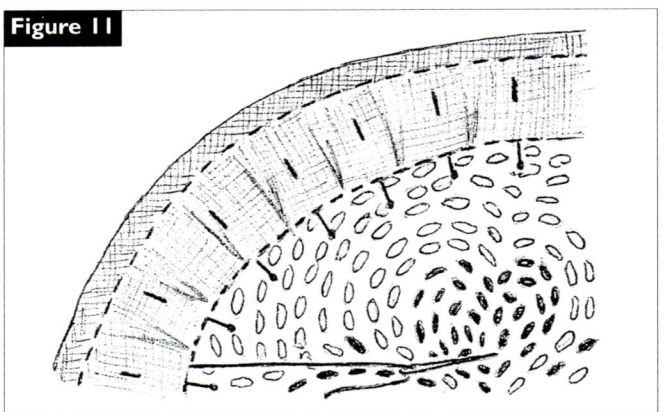

Figure 11

If your rug has rounded edges, it is helpful to baste the linen at the fold-line of your hem. Pull the basting thread tight, so that the hem lies flat against the rounded edge. Pin in place and hem.

Back of finished **Crown of Thorns** rug, showing bound edge, mitered corner, hem, and labels.

may purchase padding from a carpet store, which you can cut to fit your rug. This will keep the rug from sliding on a hardwood floor and prevent wear and tear.

Mounting A Rug on the Wall

If you wish to display your rug on the wall, you can simply install the rug on very small nails that poke through the backing but don't show on the front. The larger the rug, the more nails you will want in order to spread out the weight of the rug. Carpet strips can be very handy for this purpose. These are usually used to install wall-to-wall carpeting and can be purchased at a hardware store. They have nails coming out the back (that you will hammer into the wall). On the top of the strip, they have nails staggered about 1" apart. Gently lay your rug over the strip, and the weight will be evenly supported on the strip. If the rug is large, you can have the rug mounted on one carpet strip on the top and on another in the middle to further distribute the weight of the rug.

The Final Touches

I sew labels on the back of my rug. One label I use describes how the rug should be washed, and another label says, "Hand-hooked by Judy Taylor." If the rug is hand-spun, I also have a label that says, "Hand-spun by Judy Taylor." (To contact the company that made my labels, check the "Sources" section on page 63.)

When the hem is complete and labels sewn on, I press the edge with a steam iron on the backside of the rug. The rug can then be placed on the floor. You

Buster rug being hung on the carpet strip.

Buster rug hanging on the carpet strip.

Care, Cleaning, and Repair

Now that you have all the tools and tips to create your own yarn-hooked master-piece, feel free to let your creative spirit soar. But once that masterpiece is done, please remember that it won't clean itself or keep itself in good repair. If you want your new heirloom to last through the generations, all it takes is a few simple steps to keep it looking just like it did the day you fin-ished hooking it. See the tips below.

Vacuuming

Regular vacuuming is good for hooked rugs. If your rug is densely hooked, dirt doesn't usually go deep inside the rug, but it does collect on the top and bottom. Examine the surface of the rug, top and bottom, to make sure there are no loops that have pulled out. If not, you can safely vacuum both sides of the rug. Just don't use any of the extension hoses or brushes, as they might break some-thing loose.

Moths

It is also good to watch for wool moths, which leave a cobweb-like cocoon on the wool. If you find any cocoons, remove them and spray the rug with insecticide, or if your room has lots of wool in it, bug bomb the room. If you don't want to use insecticide, put your rug in a plastic bag and freeze it for 24 hours. This will kill any eggs. Wool moths like to lay their eggs in undisturbed locations, so regular vacuuming and cleaning is the best deterrent.

Vacuuming **Welcome Home** rug (designed and hooked by Judy Taylor).

Scrubbing **Welcome Home** rug.

Washing A Hooked Rug

The best method for cleaning a hooked rug is to scrub the surface using light pressure with a sponge, on the top and bottom of the rug. It is not necessary or recommended to get the rug soaking wet. In fact, when the pio-neers wanted to clean their rugs, they waited for a good powdery snow, took the rugs outside, put snow on top,

How I Fixed An Heirloom

I ran across the problem of damaged backing in a 65-year-old rug. Cora Laurence, the owner of this charming rug, contacted me through the shop where I teach classes in Seattle to find out if the hole in the backing could be repaired. The rug, hooked by Cora's godmother, May Horner, in 1937, had spent some time folded on a chair, and the backing became worn in that spot on the fold line. After examining the rug, I explained to Cora that I would make every effort to match the color, but that some variation is to be expected in this type of repair. She accepted that possibility, so I started on the repair job. Here's how I fixed the problem:

During repair: Backside of the rug. I unhooked the yarn around the damaged backing, and I sewed a small patch of new backing in its place. Then I tacked down all loose threads around the new backing.

into the good backing around the hole. (Even though the original backing was burlap, I decided to use linen in the patch, because it is more durable.) I tacked the patch in place, going back and forth across the damaged backing, to give the area support.

Before repair: A rug hooked by May Horner in 1937 with damaged burlap backing. Also pictured are various attempts to dye yarn to match the rug.

Step One: The yarn in May's rug appeared to be a bulky wool yarn in a warm beige color. I had a tan Halcyon yarn that seemed pretty close in color and thickness, but it was much too bright. I made a dye bath by dipping a teabag in a pot of boiling water. I continually took samples of yarn out of the dye bath, checking for the color change. After about 20 minutes, the color was getting toned down, but still the yarn seemed too bright to match the rug. I then added a little bleach to the dye bath and boiled the yarn for about 20 minutes more. By then the color seemed pretty close. I rinsed the yarn and laid it to dry while I continued with the repair. (In the picture above, from left to right, the original Halcyon yarn, the same yarn after 20 minutes in the tea dye bath, and the same yarn after 20 more minutes in the combined tea/bleach dye bath.)

Step Two: In order to patch the hole in the rug, I needed to unhook yarn all around the hole, until I came to backing that was in good shape. I then made a patch with linen, large enough to sew

After repair: May's rug restored to its previous quality.

Step Three: When the yarn was dry, I re-hooked the area, hooking through both the old backing and the patch. Since the original rug was sheared on top, I hooked my loops higher than normal, so that I would be able to trim them to the same height as the rest of the rug. When I laid the repaired rug on the floor, no one in my family could tell me where the repair was done, so I decided that it was a success. I mailed the rug back to Cora, where it now lies on a bureau in her bedroom.

swept it off, and took the rugs inside to dry! You just need enough moisture to lift the dirt off the surface.

A simple solution of a tablespoon of laundry detergent and a splash of vinegar in a few cups of water makes a good cleaner. Make sure the detergent dissolves completely, so you don't get flakes of soap on your rug. Dip a sponge in the soapy water, and squeeze it almost all the way out. Then scrub the surface of the rug in a circular motion, front and back. Periodically rinse the sponge in cold water, and go over the washed area to remove some of the soap. Then lay the rug somewhere where it can get plenty of air to dry. I use old window screens, propped up on soup cans, so the rug gets plenty of air circulation on both the top and bottom.

Warning about Dry Cleaning

Avoid dry cleaning your rugs unless your dry cleaner can assure you that he knows what he is doing! A dry cleaner with some experience cleaning hooked rugs can do a good job, but these rugs can be ruined if not handled properly, so if they must be dry cleaned, make sure your dry cleaner knows what's what! Cleaning your rugs at home is really so simple that it isn't necessary to take the risk of dry cleaning. If powdery snow was good enough for the pioneers, it's good enough for me!

Repairing Hooked Rugs

With normal wear and tear, a hooked rug will need to be repaired at some time. The most common repair is to periodically re-hook any loops that have been snagged. But after many years, some high-traffic

Welcome Home lying upside-down on a window screen to dry.

areas may become worn and need to be replaced. If the backing is in good shape, you can simply pull out the damaged area and re-hook with new yarn. You may be able to purchase yarn that is a good match, or you may need to go to the dye pot to get the color that you need. It is possible to make the repair invisible, but even if it shows up, like the patches on an old treasured quilt, the repairs will add to the charm of the rug.

Sometimes the backing of the rug can be damaged, torn, or chewed by the family pet. Fear not—you will not have to replace the family pet; even damaged backing can be replaced. Pull the loops out of the damaged area until you get to fabric that is intact. Sew a new piece of backing on the backside of the rug, tacking down as much of the damaged backing as possible. Trim away any loose threads of backing. Then re-hook the area, hooking through both layers of backing.

Hooking Other Types of Projects

Rug hooking is not just for **rugs!** This versatile craft lends itself well to all types of projects.

Stuffed animals are great fun, and hooked stuffed animals make absolutely unique gifts. I have made over 75 teddy bears, dogs, cats, dolls, geese, hobby horses, as well as hobby giraffes, alpacas, and dragons! These projects are quick and full of personality; no two animals are ever quite the same.

When I am planning a stuffed animal project, I draw my pattern pieces on burlap, leaving plenty of room between pieces (at least 4"), so the burlap won't unravel when the pieces are cut out. I hook the pieces, cut them out, and hand-sew them together. I use heavy-weight upholstery thread because I want to make sure the seams are very secure. I don't trim away the excess burlap unless I have to, and if I have to trim very close to the hooked edge, I reinforce the hooked edge with upholstery thread. I also hook my initials, the year, and the number of the animal somewhere on the hooked piece. I have a lot of fun personalizing the animals with accessories, such as glasses, hats, garments, lace, ribbons, you name it!

New Techniques for Hooked Projects

STUFFED SHEEP: In order to make a stuffed sheep that can stand up, you need to add something to make the legs

Page 52: Hooked stuffed animals, Christmas ornaments, tree skirt, Santa dummy board, rocking horse, rooster wallhanging, and pillows, all designed and hooked by Judy Taylor.

stiff. I insert wooden doweling into the legs of my sheep when I am adding the stuffing. I stuff all around the dowel and cut them long enough so that the wood sticks out of the leg piece by a couple of inches.

I then pin the legs in place on the stuffed body of the sheep. Before sewing the legs in place, I check to see that the sheep is balanced on its legs. If it wobbles, I will adjust the legs up or down until all four feet touch the ground. I sew the legs in place with heavy upholstery thread.

HOBBY HORSE: To make the mane on the hobby horse, I connect the long strands of yarn to the middle headpiece using a latch-hook technique. First, I push the hook through just one strand of the burlap.

Then, I connect with the middle of a strand of yarn, about 24" long, folded over the hook. I pull the loop through the strand of the burlap, and then I push the hook through the loop and pull the ends of the yarn through the loop.

I then pull the ends tight. When I've hooked the whole horse's head and sewn the pieces together, I trim all the ends of

CREATING A STUFFED SHEEP

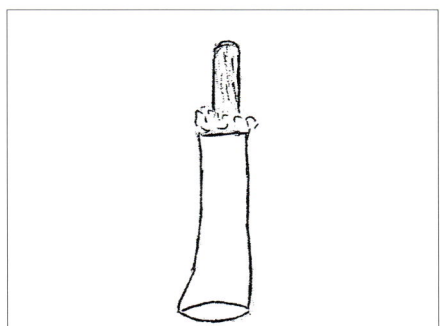

Figure 1: Doweling in stuffed leg.

Figure 2: The stuffed legs being sewn onto the stuffed body with heavy upholstery thread.

LATCH HOOKING A HOBBY HORSE MANE

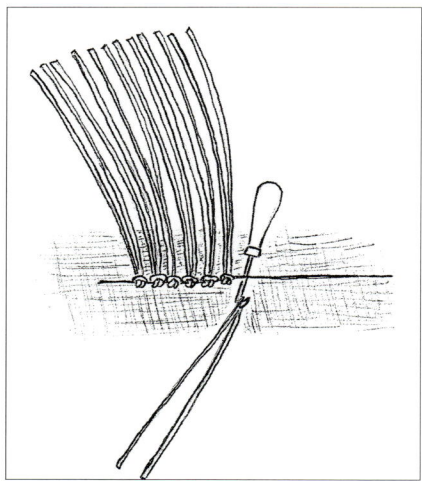

Figure 1: Hook pushed through one strand of burlap.

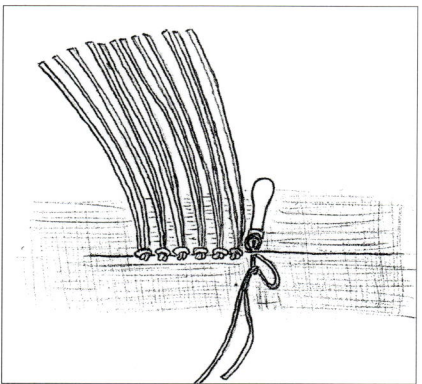

Figure 2: Hook pushed through loop, pulling ends through the loop.

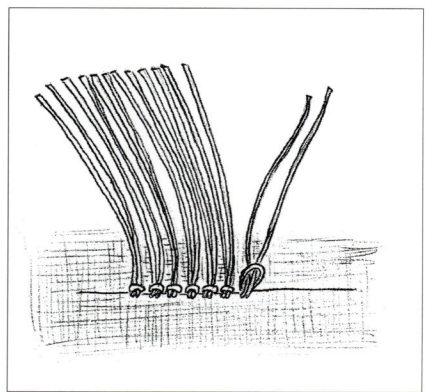

Figure 3: Pulling the ends tight.

the mane so that they are the same length, with a few shorter bangs to hang down in the front.

FIBER PLAY: Stuffed animals also allow me to play around with different hooking materials. I use softer yarns leftover from knitting projects for teddy bears, which makes them cuddlier. I also hook with locks of unspun mohair or wool for a curly effect (see Santa's beard). Mohair, Lincoln, and Border Leicester sheep have 6" long, curly locks that can be hooked without spinning. I pull up one end of the washed lock, and hook the next few loops higher than when I am hooking with yarn. I can usually hook about 3 or 4 loops per lock. I don't trim the ends right down to the surface, but leave about $1/2$" sticking up. These types of wool fleece come in many natural colors, so the Santa beard could be pure white, gray, red, or black. The curly effect is also great for hooking stuffed sheep and poodles.

Making Holiday Ornaments

Hooked holiday ornaments are charming decorations, and they are a snap to make. I try to make ornaments that are about 3" in length, so they will hang nicely on the tree.

To make the sheep ornaments, I draw ovals with funny faces on them and hook the faces black and the bodies white (or sometimes gray or brown). I cut the sheep out of the burlap and tack down the edges to the back with a needle and thread. I trim away as much burlap as I can, so it won't be too bulky in the back.

At this point I sew in some decorative thread in the top to hang the ornament. I measure out 3" pieces of pipe cleaner, which I fold over in the middle. I hot

Holiday ornaments, **Sheep** and **Santa**, shown from front and back.

glue the pipe cleaner legs onto the back, so about 1" of pipe cleaner sticks out the bottom. Then I hot glue felt to the back. When the glue cools, I trim the excess felt away from the back.

To make the Santas, I hook the simple faces with yarn; then I hook the beard with unspun locks of washed mohair. I hook the mohair loops higher than the yarn, which makes a curlier effect. I leave both ends of the mohair locks sticking out, rather than trimming them, which also adds to the curliness. (If the ends seem frizzy, I will trim them a bit and add a little water to make the ends curl again.) I then cut out the Santas and tack the edges down to the back, just as with the sheep ornament. I sew decorative thread in the top to hang the ornament; then I hot glue felt to the back. When the glue cools, I trim away the excess felt.

Four Projects for You to Try

Now that you have a comprehension of the basics of hooking with yarn, I felt it was only fitting to conclude the book with four projects to try on your own. Feel free to hook these designs using my suggested colors in each section, or go wild and make your own colorful design using the tips and techniques in the book.

Just remember to make the projects uniquely your own. And of course, don't forget the most important rule in rug hooking and hooking with yarn: Have fun!

Instructions for *Welcome Sheep*

Reynolds Lopi or Brown Sheep Lamb's Pride Lopi works well for this wallhanging. This is also a good project for using up leftover scraps, since you only need a little of each color.

Yarn Needed:

- **Sheep:** 1 oz.
- **Sheep faces:** A small amount.
- **Inner background:** 1 oz.
- **Welcome section background:** 2 oz.
- **Outer Background:** 2 oz.
- **Lettering and outline:** 1 oz.

Welcome Sheep, 19" x 10", Brown Sheep Lopi on burlap. Designed and hooked by Judy Taylor, Auburn, Washington, 2001.

Birdhouses, 27" x 11 1/2", Reynolds Lopi on burlap. Designed and hooked by Judy Taylor, Auburn, Washington, 2000.

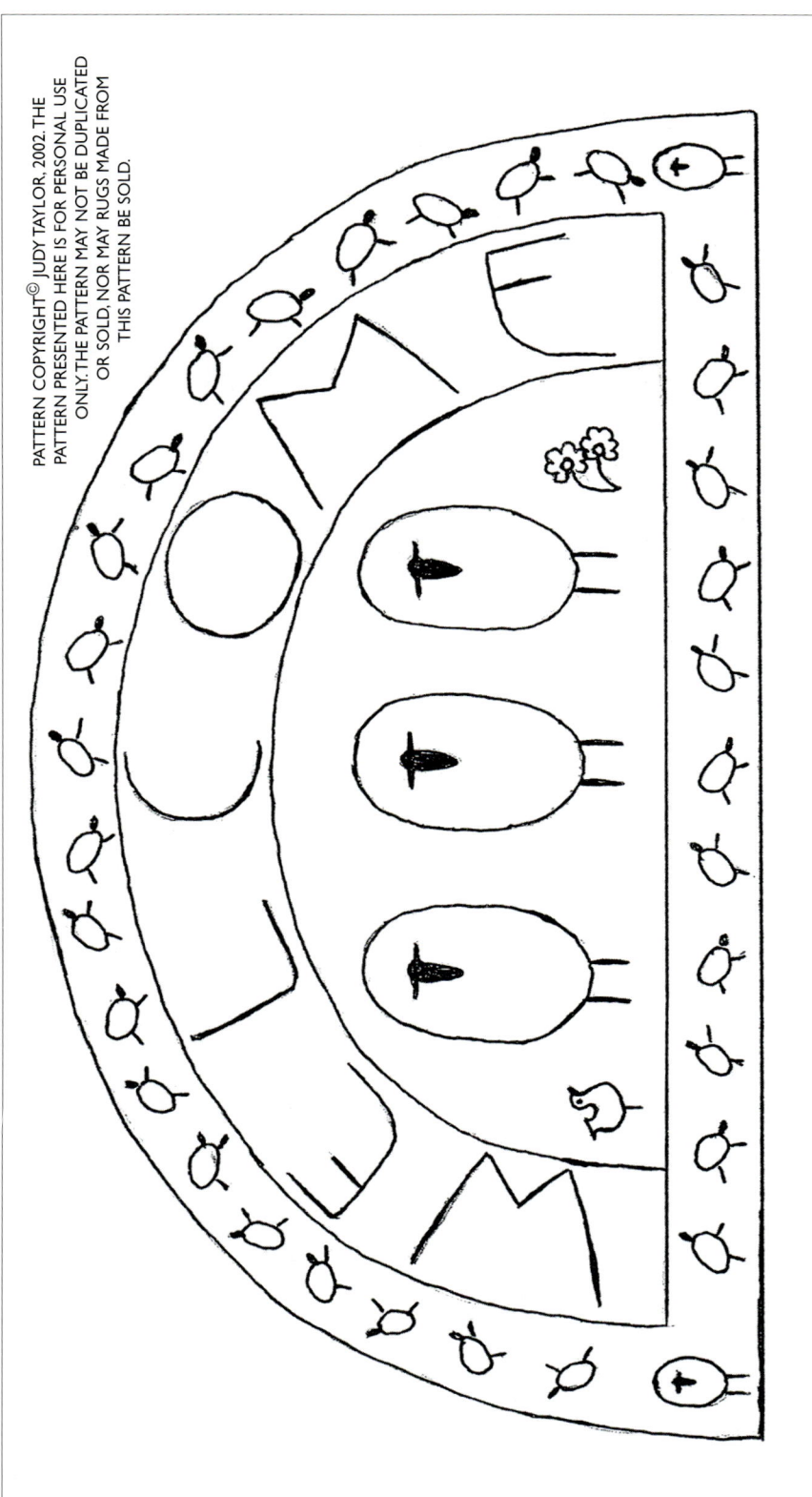

This wallhanging was inspired by Mary Engelbreit's wonderful designs, so I chose bright, whimsical colors. I have done this pattern in a whole variety of color schemes, depending on the décor of the room in which it was intended to hang. Practically any color combination would work for this design. You can do three white sheep with black faces, but I have also done this design with one white sheep with a black face, a gray sheep with a black face, and a light brown sheep with a dark brown face.

Incorporate your initials and the year somewhere in the design, if desired. When you are done hooking, do a simple folded hem. In order to turn the rounded edge under without bunching the fabric in the back, baste along the fold line on the round part of the rug. Pull the basting thread tight, and pin the hem in place. Taking deep stitches, so you are sure to sew through the backing and not just the yarn, hem the wallhanging. You can easily hang this rug on the wall with two small nails, gently pushing the nails through the backing.

Instructions for Birdhouses

Reynolds Lopi and Brown Sheep Lamb's Pride Bulky Lopi work well for this type of wallhanging. The birdhouses and sunflowers can be decorated with leftovers in a "hit or miss" pattern.

Yarn Needed:

- **Birdhouses:** figure about 4 oz. for each birdhouse, in several colors, for a total of around 16 oz.
- **Background:** 10 oz.
- **Sunflowers:** small amounts of yellow, gold, and green

This is another type of wallhanging that can be hooked in a whimsical way. Just about any color scheme will work. When I have hooked the birdhouses in wild, kooky colors, I hooked the background with a solid-colored yarn. In another version, I hooked the birdhouses in a red, white, and blue theme, so I used a variegated yarn in the background for extra visual interest. If desired, hook your initials and the year in the design. When you are finished hooking, fold the hem under and sew it to the back, making sure you take deep stitches, so you are connecting the backing and not just the yarn. To hang this rug on a wall, hammer three or four tiny nails on the wall, and gently push the rug onto the nails.

Instructions for Hooking a *Shaded Rose*

New Zealand Wool Pak works really well for the dip-dyed yarn (please see Chapter 7 for instructions on wrapping and dip-dyeing skeins), and Brown Sheep Lopi or Reynolds Lopi works well for the background.

The key to making a hooked rose look like a rose is to create a contrast between the highlight at the outside end of a petal and the lowlight, or the shadow at the base of the petal beneath it.

Beginning at the darker end of the dip-dyed strand, hook each petal from the inside to the outside, always hooking in the same direction (inside of the petal to the outside).

I don't necessarily start with the very darkest end of the strand. I often pull the end up and hook a few loops before deciding whether I'm going to get to the faded end of the strand by the outside

PATTERN COPYRIGHT© JUDY TAYLOR. 2002. THE PATTERN PRESENTED HERE IS FOR PERSONAL USE ONLY. THE PATTERN MAY NOT BE DUPLICATED OR SOLD, NOR MAY RUGS MADE FROM THIS PATTERN BE SOLD.

Birdhouses, 27" x 11¹/₂", Halcyon yarn on burlap. Designed and hooked by Judy Taylor, Auburn, Washington, 2000.

Shaded Rose, 8" in diameter, New Zealand Wool Pak and Brown Sheep Lopi on burlap. Designed and hooked by Judy Taylor, Auburn, Washington, 2002.

end of the petal. At the same time, I want my loops at the inside of the petal to contrast with the petal above it.

It is probably best to hook the rose from the inside out. (The spot in the center is just shadow, without going for the shading effect.) Don't worry if while you are hooking the rose, it doesn't seem like a rose. You really have to hook the whole thing, cut off all the ends, and look at it from a distance. What seem like abstract blobs of color up close may surprise you when you see it from afar. The contrast between highlight and lowlight is really just an optical illusion. Much like an impressionist painting, the details add up to a familiar picture, even though up close they don't have quite the same effect.

Once observed from a distance, you can then decide if you have enough highlight and lowlight to make the rose clear. You can add a few loops of color to the shadow or highlight if you feel that they need a boost.

58

PATTERN COPYRIGHT© JUDY TAYLOR, 2002. THE PATTERN PRESENTED HERE
IS FOR PERSONAL USE ONLY. THE PATTERN MAY NOT BE DUPLICATED OR
SOLD, NOR MAY RUGS MADE FROM THIS PATTERN BE SOLD.

Hooking the Leaves

Begin in the center of a leaf, hooking with the darkest end of the strand. Keep radiating out from the center of the leaf to the outside, dark to light. I find that if I occasionally bring a dark line out further than the rest, or bring a light-colored line further in toward the center of the leaf, it gives more definition to the leaf.

Yarn Needed:

- **Rose:** 2 hanks, 40 wraps each, dip-dyed and cut on both ends
- **Leaves:** 1 hank, 30 wraps, dip-dyed and cut on both ends
- **Background:** 2 oz.

Finishing Your *Shaded Rose*

Hook the background, and if desired, incorporate your initials and the year in the design. To hem a round piece, baste stitch along the fold line of the hem. Pull the basting thread tight, and pin the hem in place. Take deep hemming stitches so that you are sure to catch the burlap backing and not just the yarn.

This project could be a decoration for a tabletop, a small wallhanging, or a

Primitive Flower Mat, 11" x 11",
Ewenique yarn on burlap. Designed and
hooked by Judy Taylor, Auburn,
Washington, 2002.

pillow. If desired, expand the design for a pillow with a border to make it larger. After it is hooked, trim the burlap and turn the extra selvage under (no need to baste at the fold line if you are making a pillow), and tack it in place to the back-ing, taking deep stitches so you are sure to grab the burlap backing and not just the yarn. For the back piece for a hooked pillow, I like to use heavy uphol-stery fabric, which is just about as stiff as the hooked side (otherwise, the back doesn't hold the shape as well). I fold under the edges of the upholstery fabric and pin the hooked side to the fabric. I hand sew all around the edges with heavy upholstery thread. I stuff my pillows with polyester stuffing because it holds its shape very well over time. If desired, decorative cording can be sewn on the outside edge to give the pillow a professional look.

Instructions for Hooking the *Primitive Flower Mat*

Yarn Needed:

- **Flowers:** 1 oz. each of pink, light gold, and dark gold, plus $^1/2$ oz. of persimmon for flower centers.
- **Leaves and stems:** 1 oz. light green, $^1/2$ oz. medium green
- **Background:** 3 oz.
- **Outline:** $^1/2$ oz. each of light green and medium green

Overdye light gray or light brown yarn for variegated effect (for instructions on dyeing variegated yarns for primitive rugs, see Chapter 6). Choose earth tones like brown, green, gold, red, and pink. To get the most of my variegated yarns, I hook the design in continuous rows, following the contours of the design elements. That way as the color changes in the yarn, it echoes the design.

If desired, hook your initials and the year somewhere in the mat. For a table-top mat or wallhanging, fold the hem under, and taking deep stitches, sew the selvage to the backing (making sure you are connecting your needle to the burlap backing, not to yarn). If you would like to make the mat into a pillow, turn your

burlap selvage under and tack into place. Use a heavy upholstery fabric for the back, so it will hold its shape. Turn the edges of the upholstery fabric under and pin to the hooked piece. Hand-sew with heavy upholstery thread, and stuff with polyester stuffing.

The following is a list of suggested sources for the many products recommended in this book. Keep in mind that this is only a partial list of the many companies that sell these products. Most of these companies, and many more, advertise in *Rug Hooking* magazine. I find that the Internet is also a fabulous resource. This list is only the beginning! These companies can get you started with all the supplies you will need to create treasured heirloom rugs. The rest is up to you! Enjoy!

	YARN	NIDDY-NODDY, SEIN-WINDER, BALL-WINDER	DYES	FRAMES	HOOKS	BACKING	PATTERNS
Creative Fibers 5416 Penn Avenue S. Minneapolis, MN 55419 (612) 927-8307 *www.creativefiber.com*	✦		✦	✦	✦	✦	✦
Edeldal Farm PO Box 2003 Auburn, WA 98071 (253) 939-1350 *edeldalfarm@earthlink.net*	✦		✦	✦	✦	✦	✦
Forestheart Studio 200 S. Main St. Box 112 Woodsboro, MD 21798 (301) 845-4447	✦		✦	✦	✦	✦	
Jane Olson Rug Studio PO Box 351 Hawthorne, CA 90250 (310) 643-5902 *www.janeolsonrugstudio.com*			✦	✦	✦	✦	✦
Liziana Creations 515 John Fitch Blvd. PO Box 59 S. Windsor, CT 06074 (860) 290-8619 *www.liziana.com*			✦	✦	✦	✦	✦
Rug Hooking, Etc. 409 N. Mall St. Lafayette, LA 70503 (877) 993-7847 *www.rughookingetc.com*	✦	✦		✦		✦	
Bountiful 211 Green Mountain Dr. Livermore, CO 80536 (877) 586-9332 *www.bountifulspinweave.com*	✦	✦					
Fredericksburg Rugs 231 Rocky Creek Rd. PO Box 649 Fredericksburg, TN 78624 (800) 331-5213 *www.fredericksburgrugs.com*			✦	✦	✦	✦	✦

	YARN	NIDDY NODDY, SEIN-WINDER, BALL-WINDER	DYES	FRAMES	HOOKS	BACKING	PATTERNS9
Joan Moshimer, **Cushing & Co.** PO Box 351 Kennebunkport, ME 04046 (800) 626-7847 *www.wcushing.com*	🐦		🐦	🐦	🐦	🐦	🐦
Carolina Homespun 455 Lisbon St. San Francisco, CA 94112 (800) 450-7786 *www.carolinahomespun.com*	🐦	🐦	🐦				
Halcyon Yarn 12 School St. Bath, ME 04530 (800) 341-0282 *www.halcyonyarn.com*	🐦	🐦	🐦	🐦	🐦	🐦	🐦
Red Clover P.O. Box 243 Cheshire, OR 97419 (800) 858-9276	🐦		🐦	🐦	🐦	🐦	🐦
Stonehill Spinning Ltd. 104 A E. Ufer Fredericksburg, TX 78624 (877) 990-8952 *www.stonehillspin.com*	🐦		🐦	🐦	🐦	🐦	🐦
Weaving Works 4717 Brooklyn Ave. NE Seattle, WA 98105 (888) 524-1221 *www.weavingworks.com*	🐦	🐦	🐦				
Woodland Woolworks 100 E. Washington St. Carlton, OR 97111 (800) 547-3725 *www.woodlandwoolworks.com*	🐦	🐦	🐦				
The Woolery 117 E. Main St. Murfreesboro, NC 27855 (800) 441-9665 *www.woolery.com*		🐦	🐦	🐦	🐦	🐦	
Yarn Barn 930 Massachusetts Laurence, KS 66044 (800) 468-0035 *www.yarnbarn-ks.com*	🐦	🐦	🐦				

Check Rug Hooking magazine to find many more suppliers of yarn, wool, and other fine hooking products. My rug labels were made by Sterling Name Tape Company, 9 Willow St., PO Box 939, Winsted, CT 06098, (800) 654-5210, www.sterlingtape.com.